Jalal al-Din Muhammad Rumi

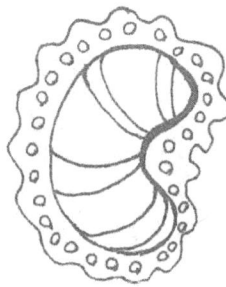

One of the great souls, as well as one of the great and ancient spiritual teachers. He was born on September 30, 1207 C. E. in Balkh Province, Afghanistan, at the time the eastern edge of the Persian Empire. Rumi descended from a long line of Islamic jurists, theologians, and mystics, including his father, who was known by followers of Rumi as "Sultan of the Scholars." When Rumi was still a young man, his father led their family more than 2,000 miles west to avoid the invasion of Genghis Khan's armies. They settled in present-day Turkey, where Rumi lived and wrote most of his life. Rumi died on December 17, 1273 C. E., in Konya, Turkey.
(Fragments of Rumi's bio taken from poets.org)

The quotes that inspired this Coloring book have been taken from:
THE ESSENTIAL RUMI
Translation by
Coleman Barks.
Harper Collins Publishers.

This coloring book is for anyone who wants to develop, discover or practice their artistic ability and creativity through coloring; it is also a space for those who seek mental relaxation and emotional discovery through coloring while inspired on Rumi's spiritual phrases that serve as guides in the path to personal empowerment.

The art of coloring, together with meditation and internalization of these inspirational phrases, will take you on a spiritual journey that relaxes your mind and spirit.

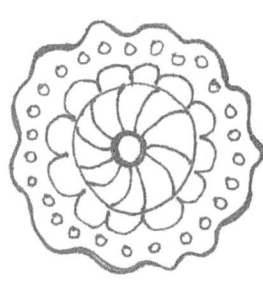

Design and illustrations by Pilar Jimenez
Copyright © 2018

AUTHOR'S NOTE
This is an invitation to share the results of your art work with the world #readpaintlove @pilarjimenez.art, and encourage others to join this magnificent journey.

Available on Amazon.com and other book stores

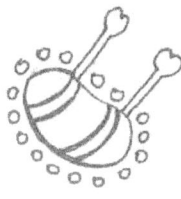

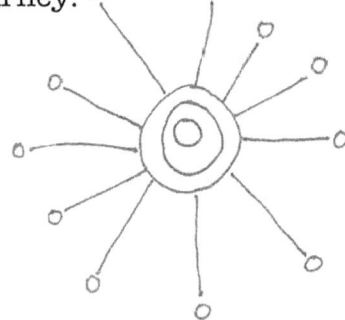

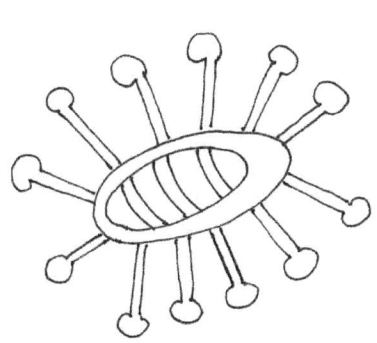 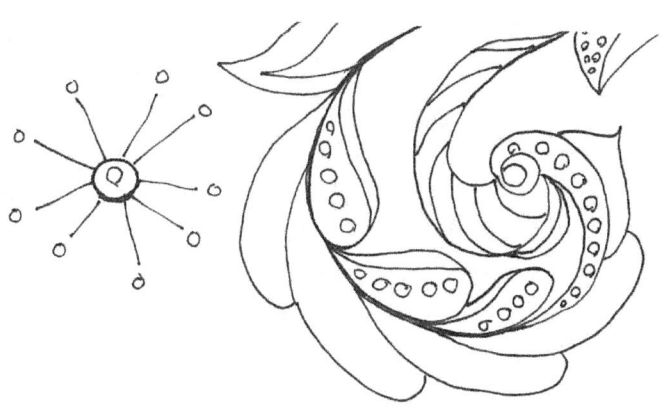

Pilar Jiménez is an American artist (born in Colombia). She holds a Communications Degree from the Xaverian University in Bogota, and graduate studies in fine arts with the most prestigious artists in Colombia as well as the Corcoran College of Art + Design in Washington DC.

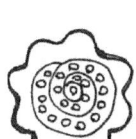 Her studies and artistic trajectory of more than 40 years combined with her passion and dedication to spiritual studies from both Western and Eastern cultures which she cultivated from an early age, led her into the process of developing spiritual and emotional healing techniques through art.

Jiménez work has been shown locally in different cities of the United States and internationally in several European and Latin American countries. Most of her pieces are now part of numerous public and private collections around the world.

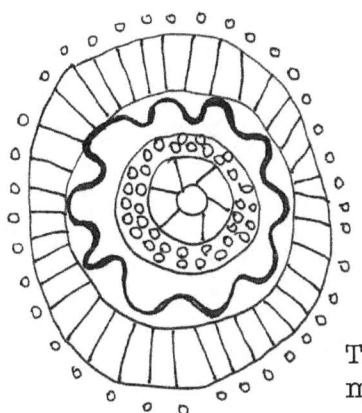 As her art work represent the unification of her two passions, art and spirituality, Pilar Jiménez decided to create this compilation of drawings of her authorship, inspired by Jalal ad-DinMuhammad Rumi, mystic poet and thinker whose work is an invitation to discover our inner beauty as well as the world that surrounds us.

This coloring book has been created as an alternative to combine meditation and self-reflection through the art of coloring.

She lives and works in her private studio in New York.

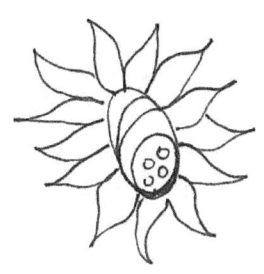 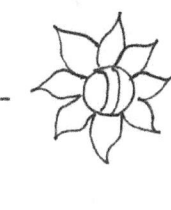 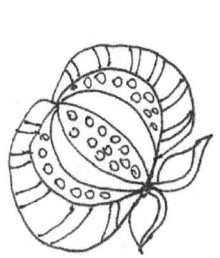 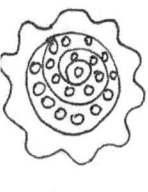

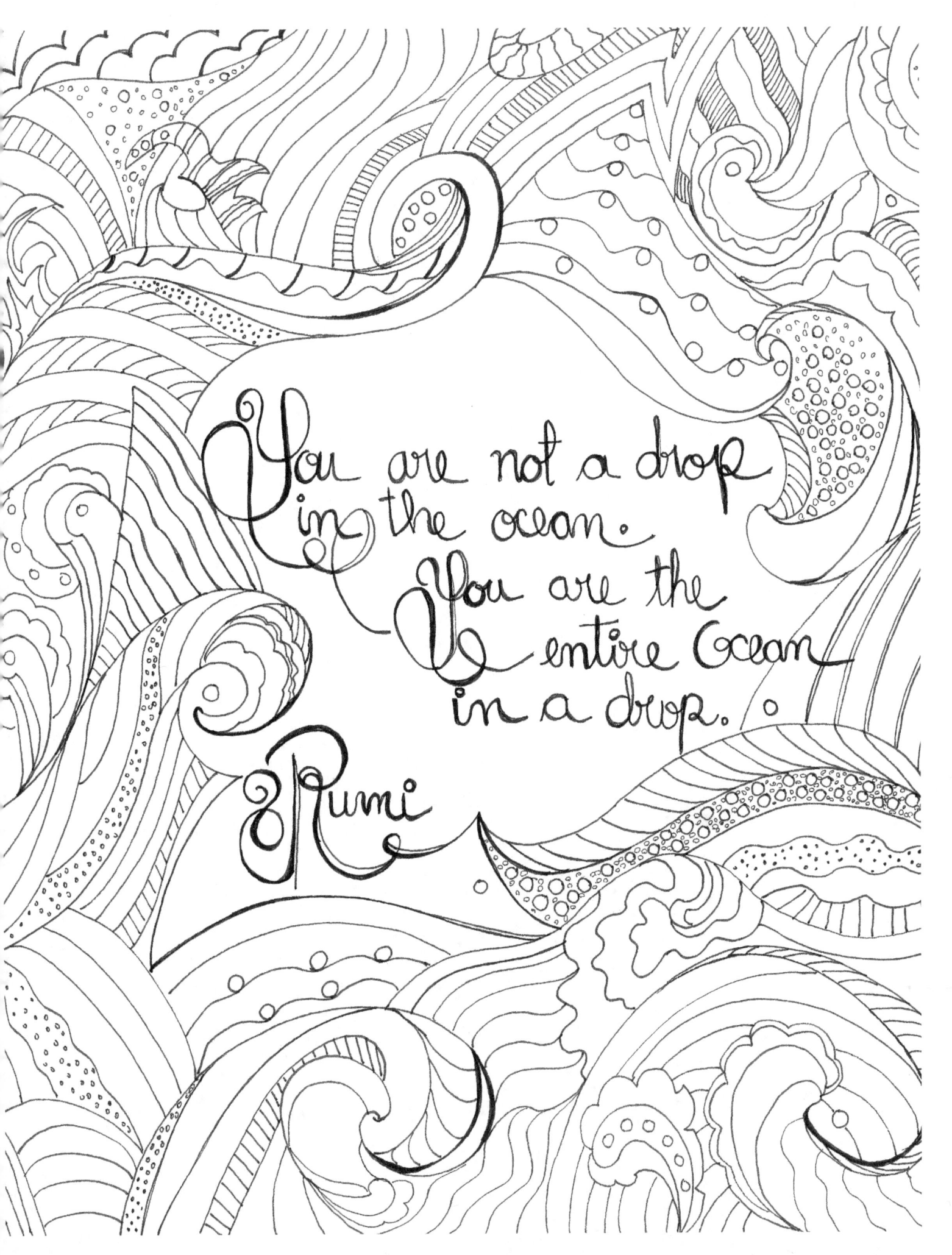

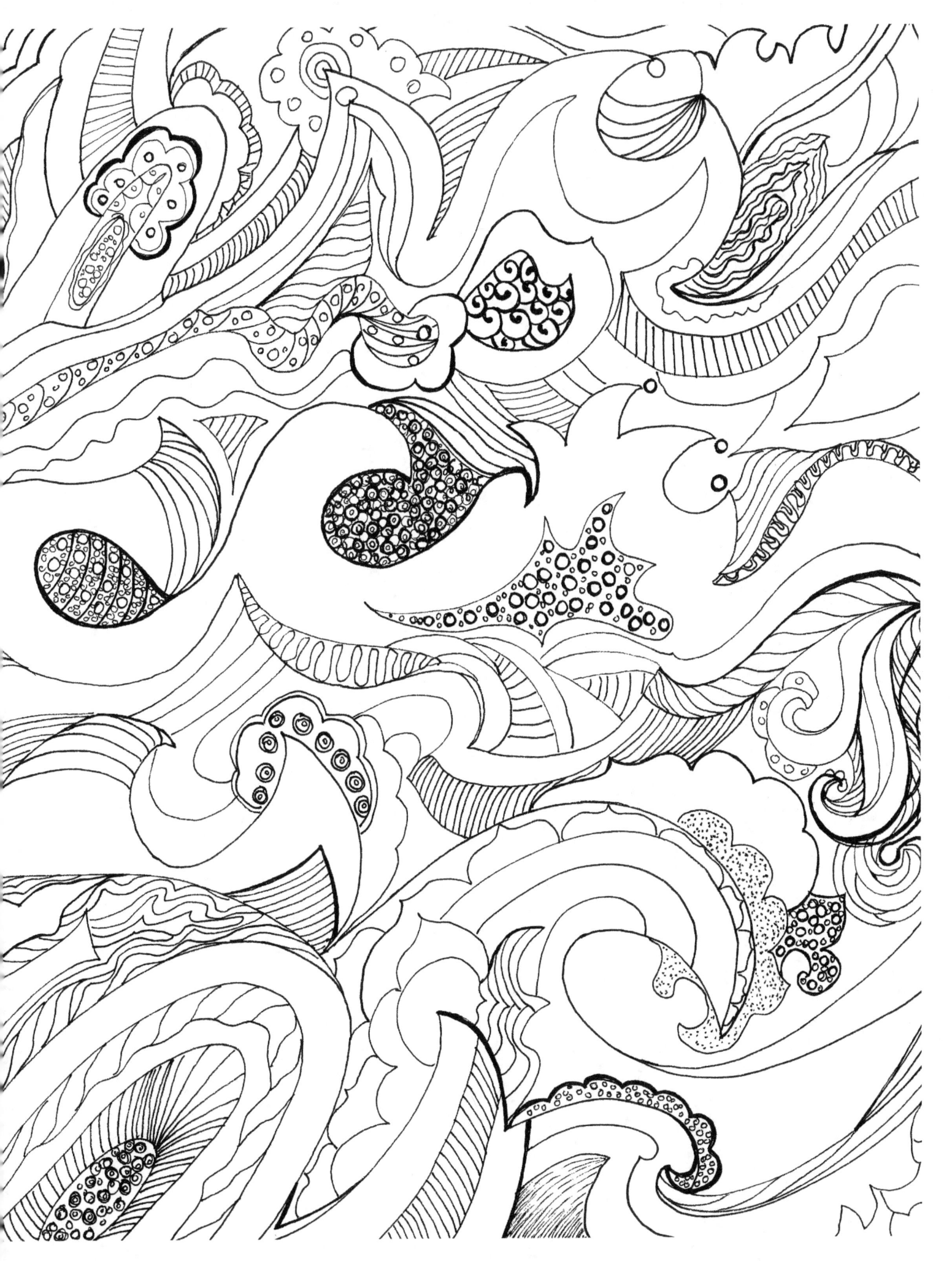

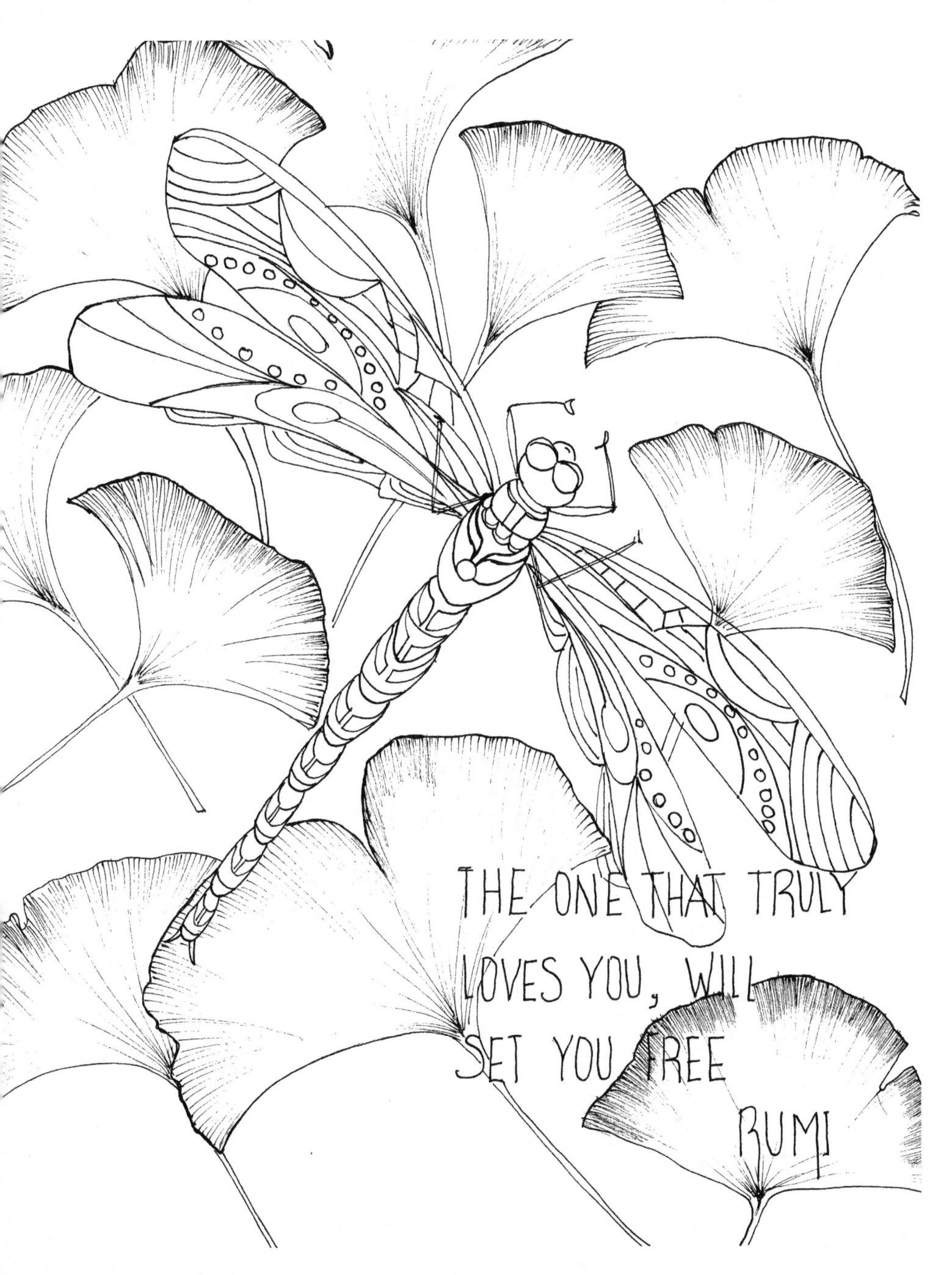

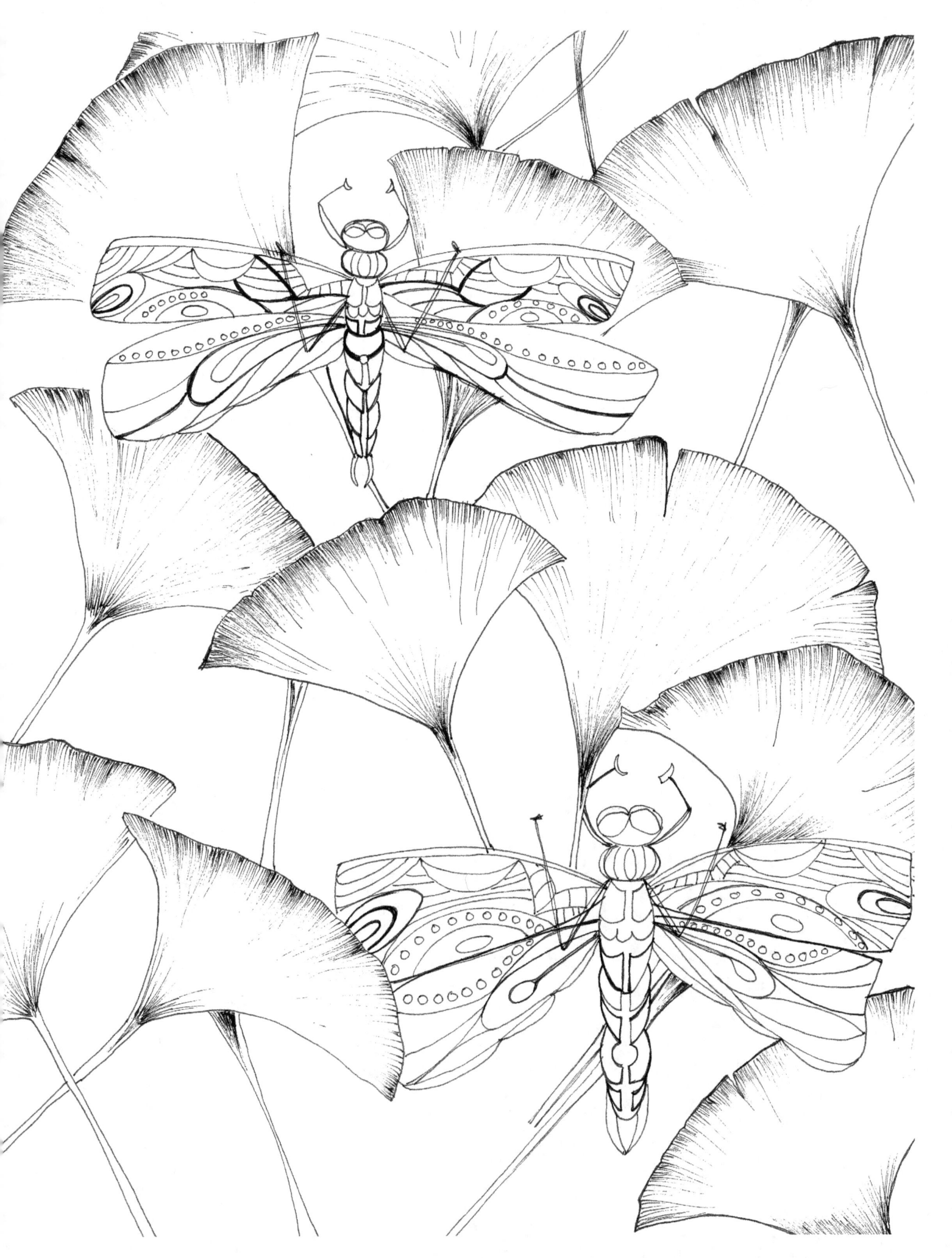

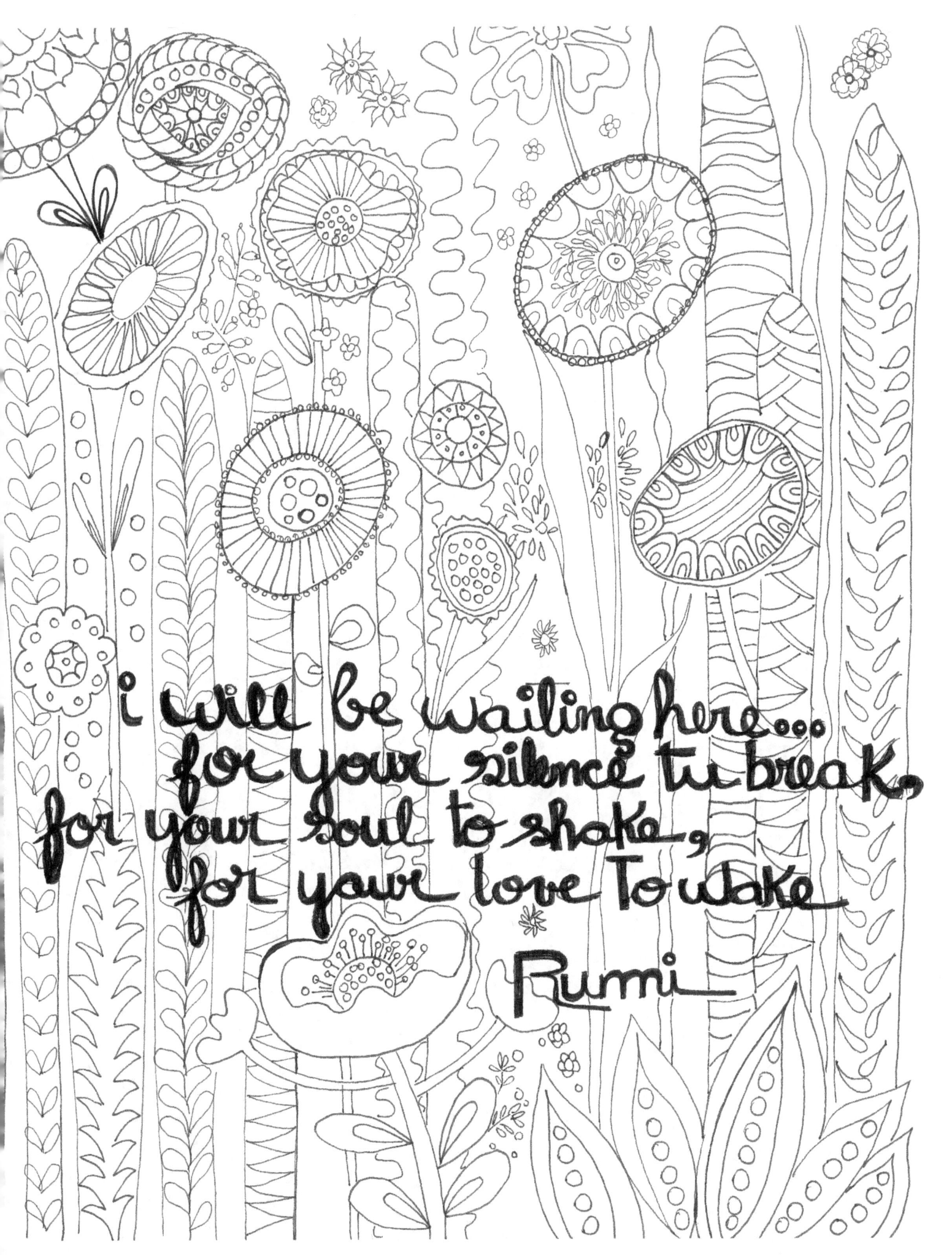

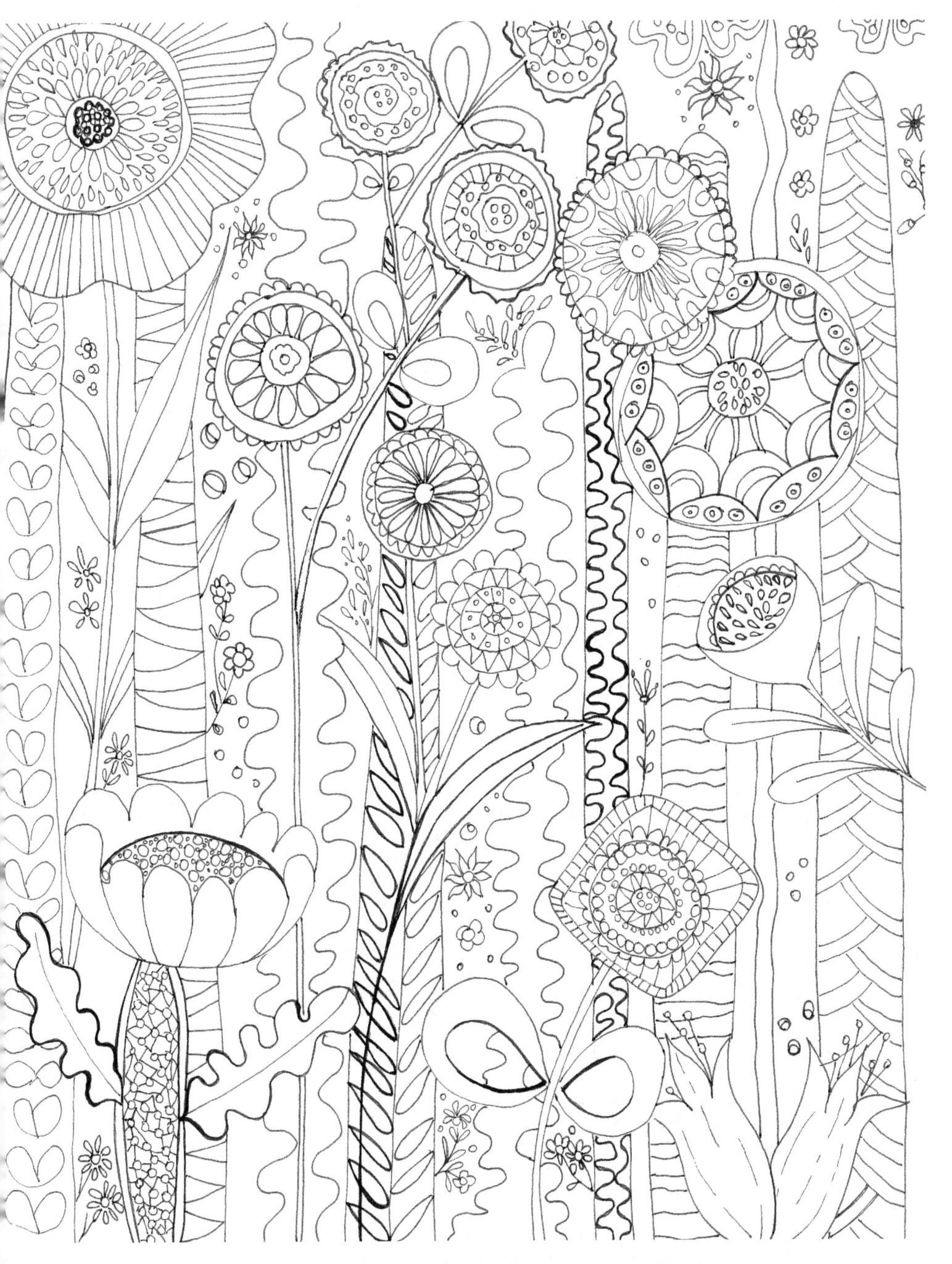

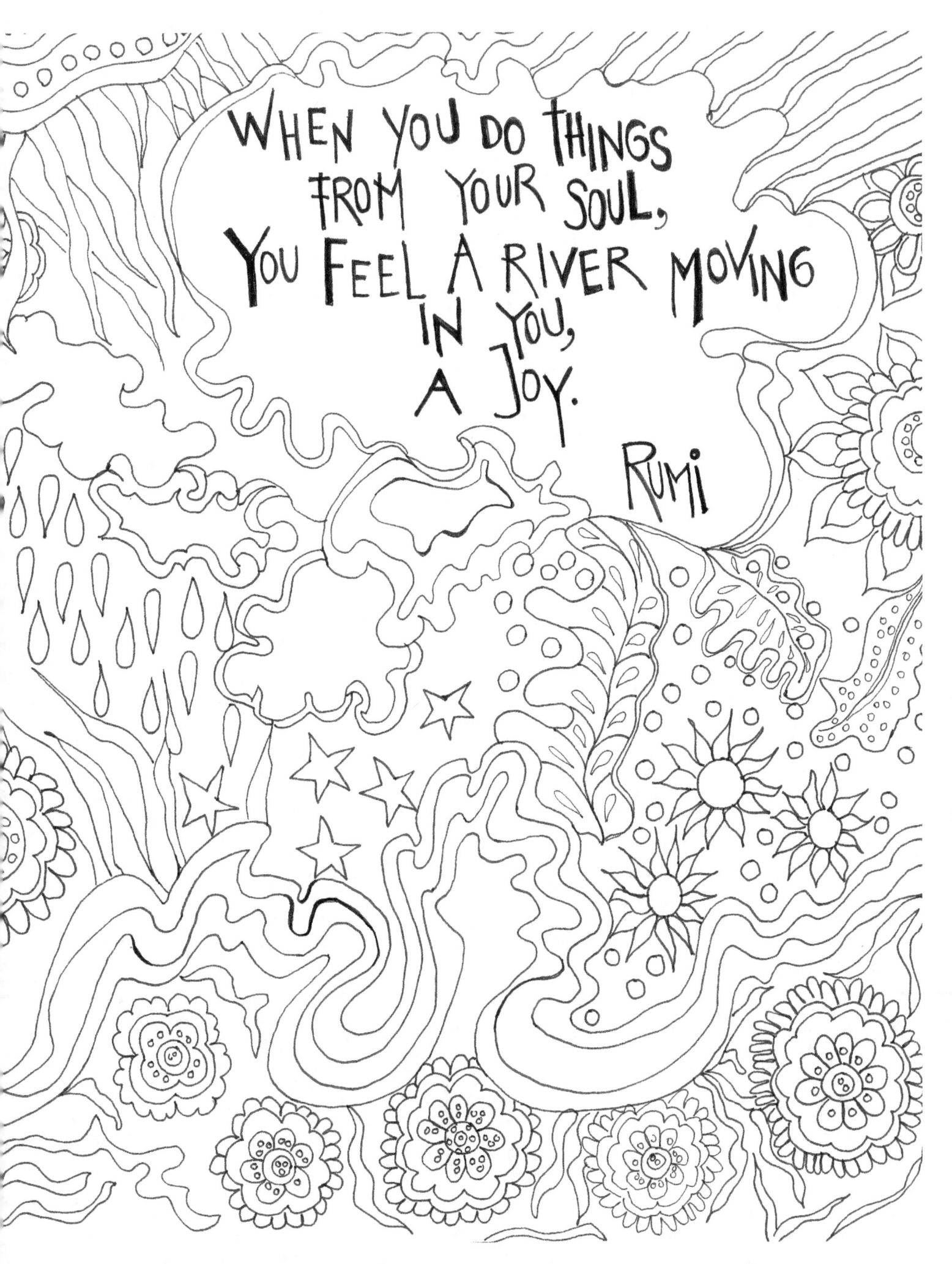

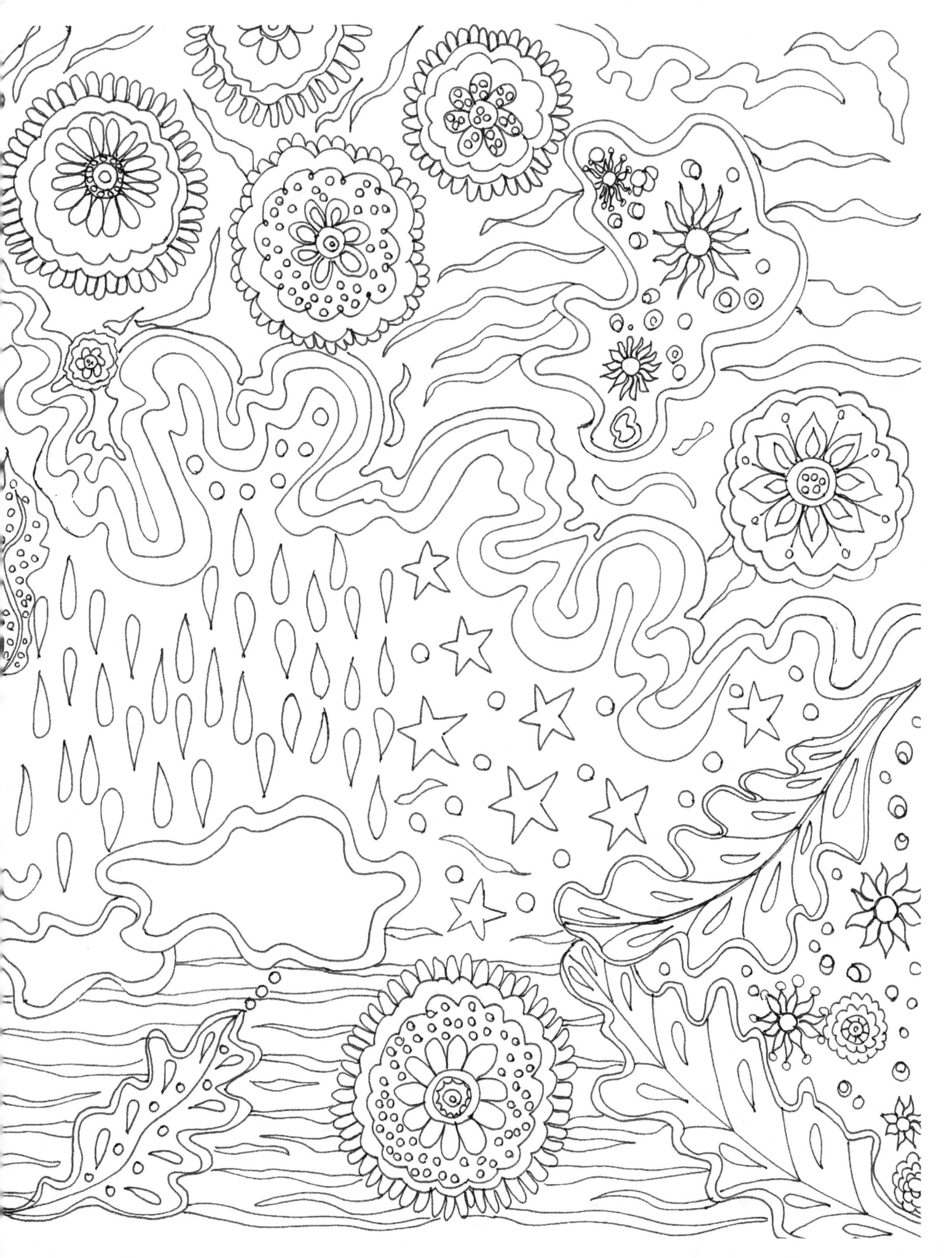

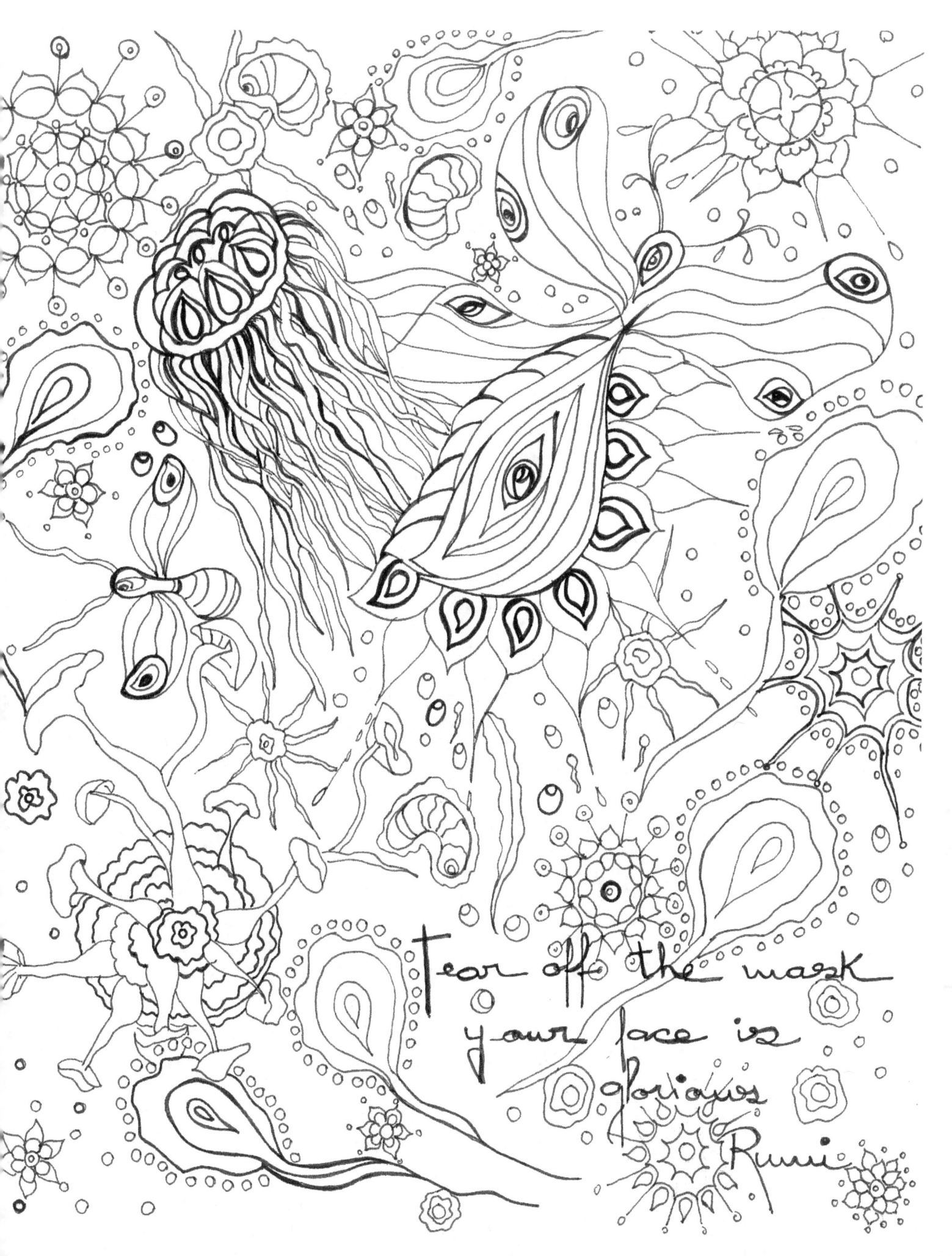

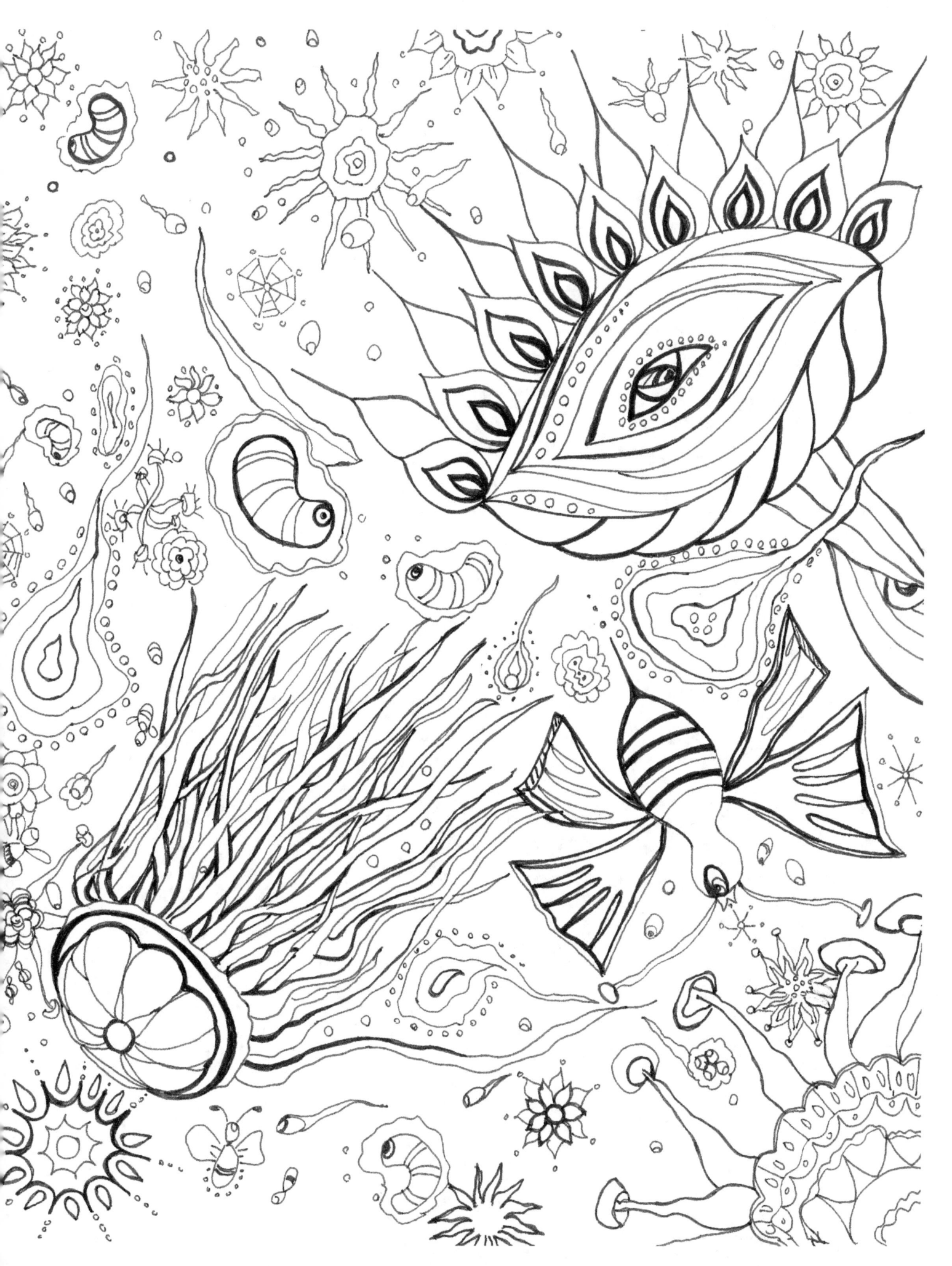

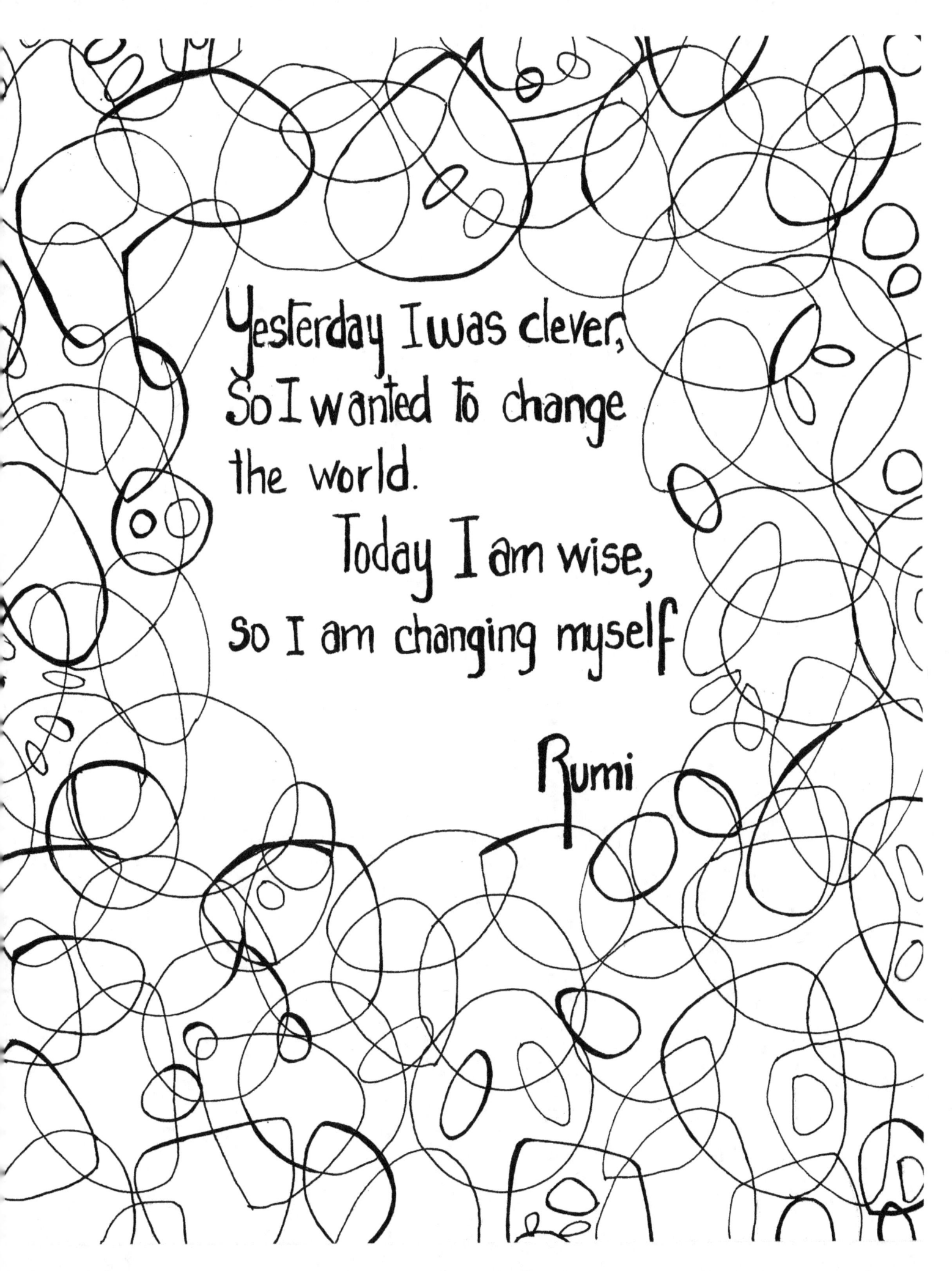

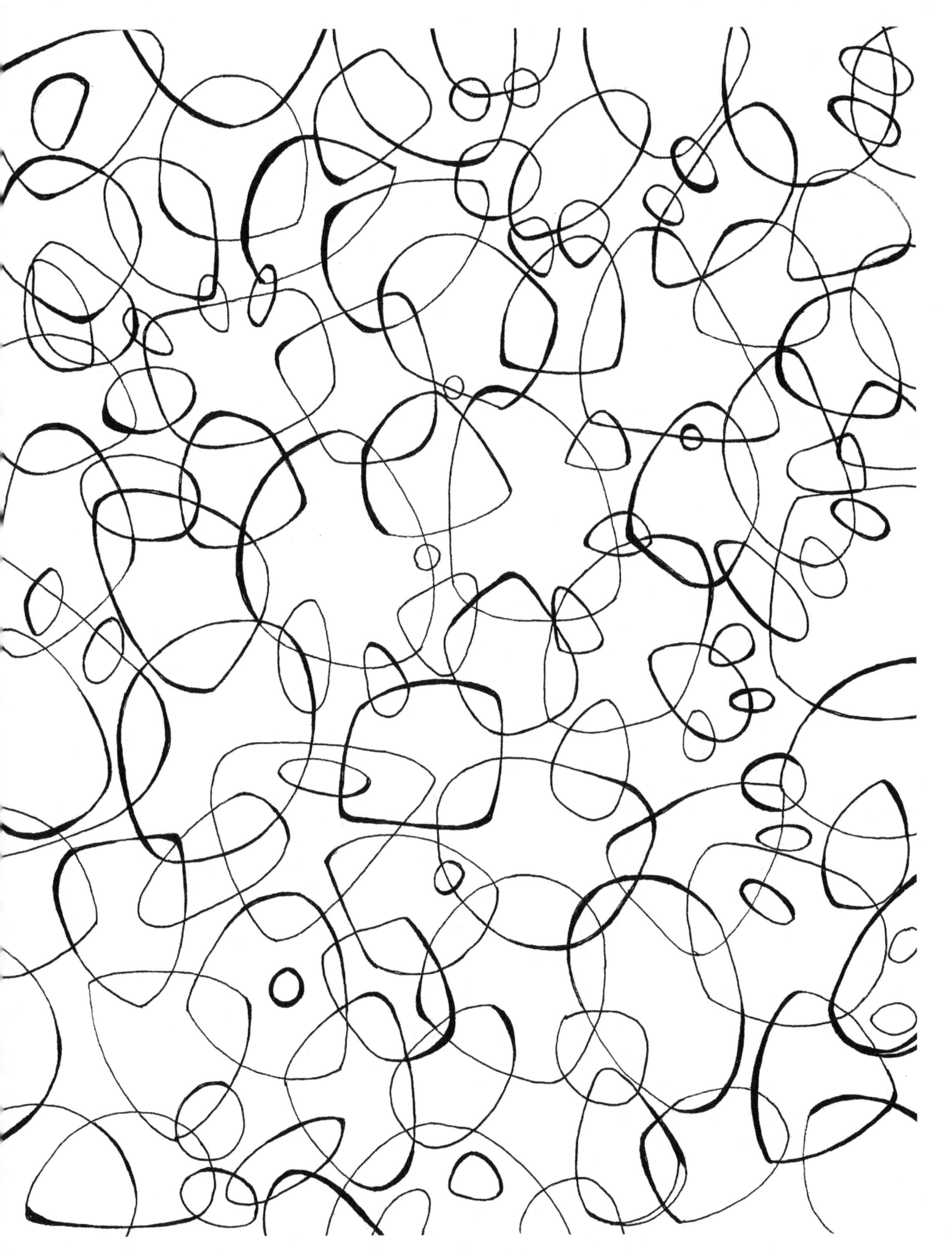

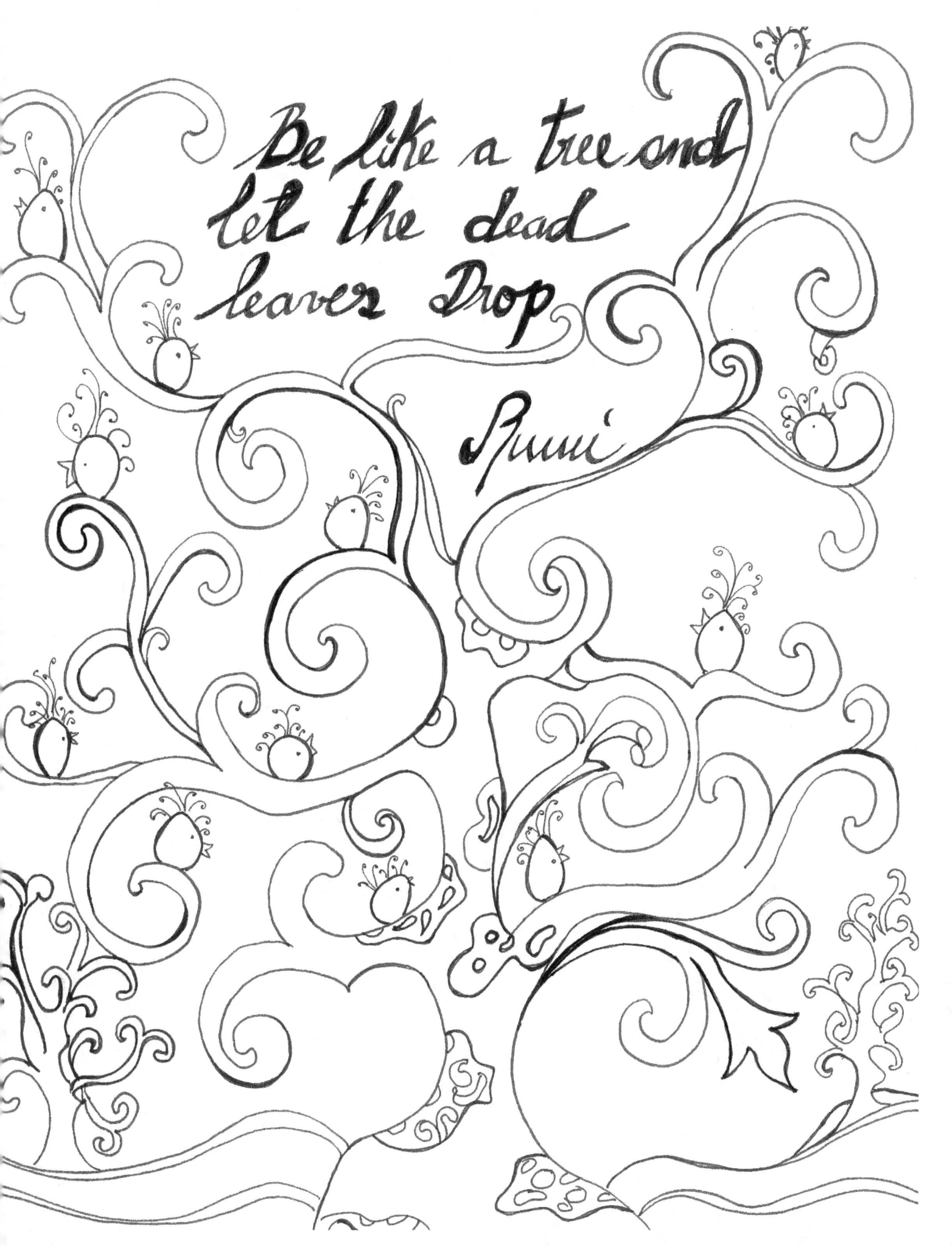

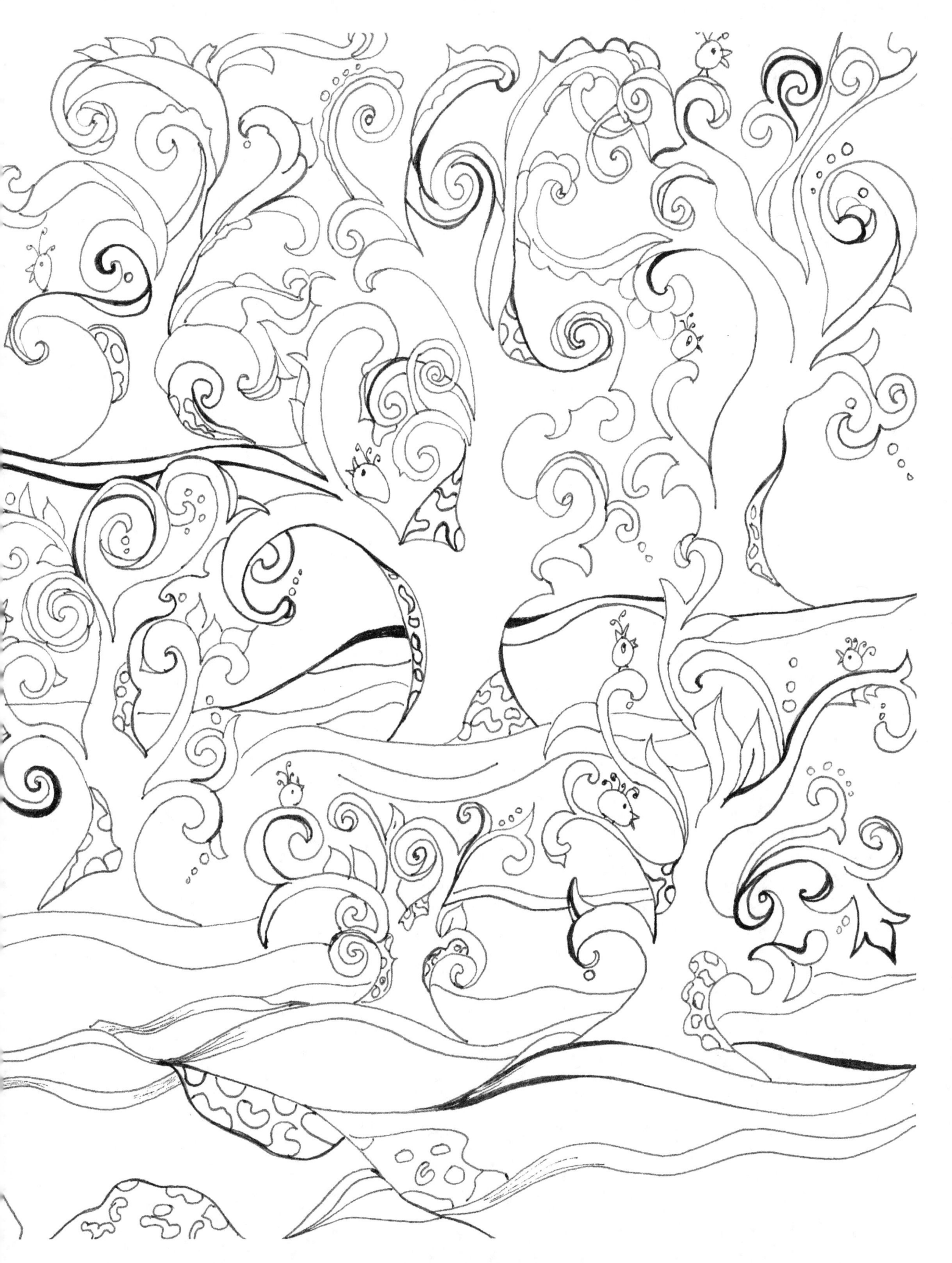

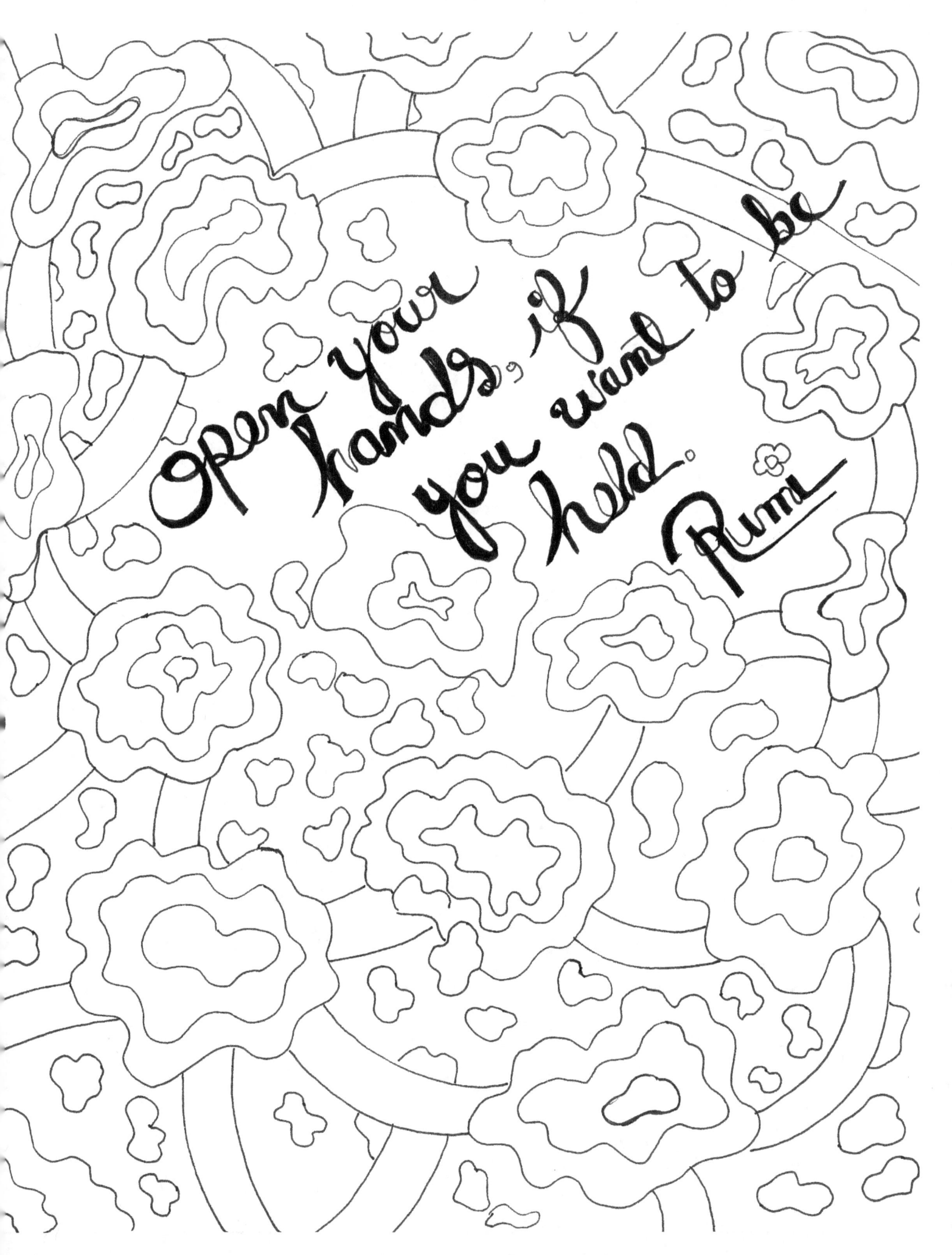

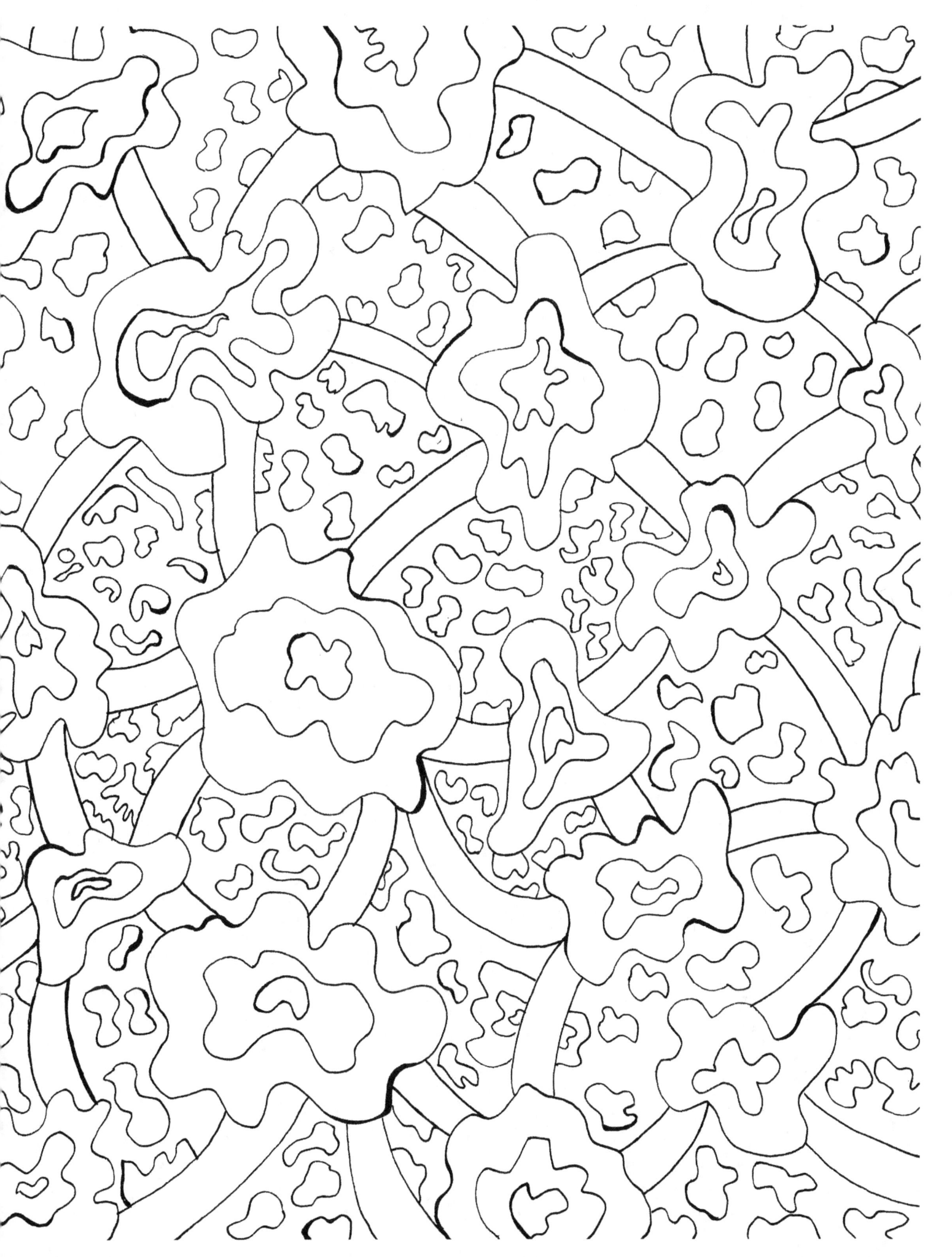

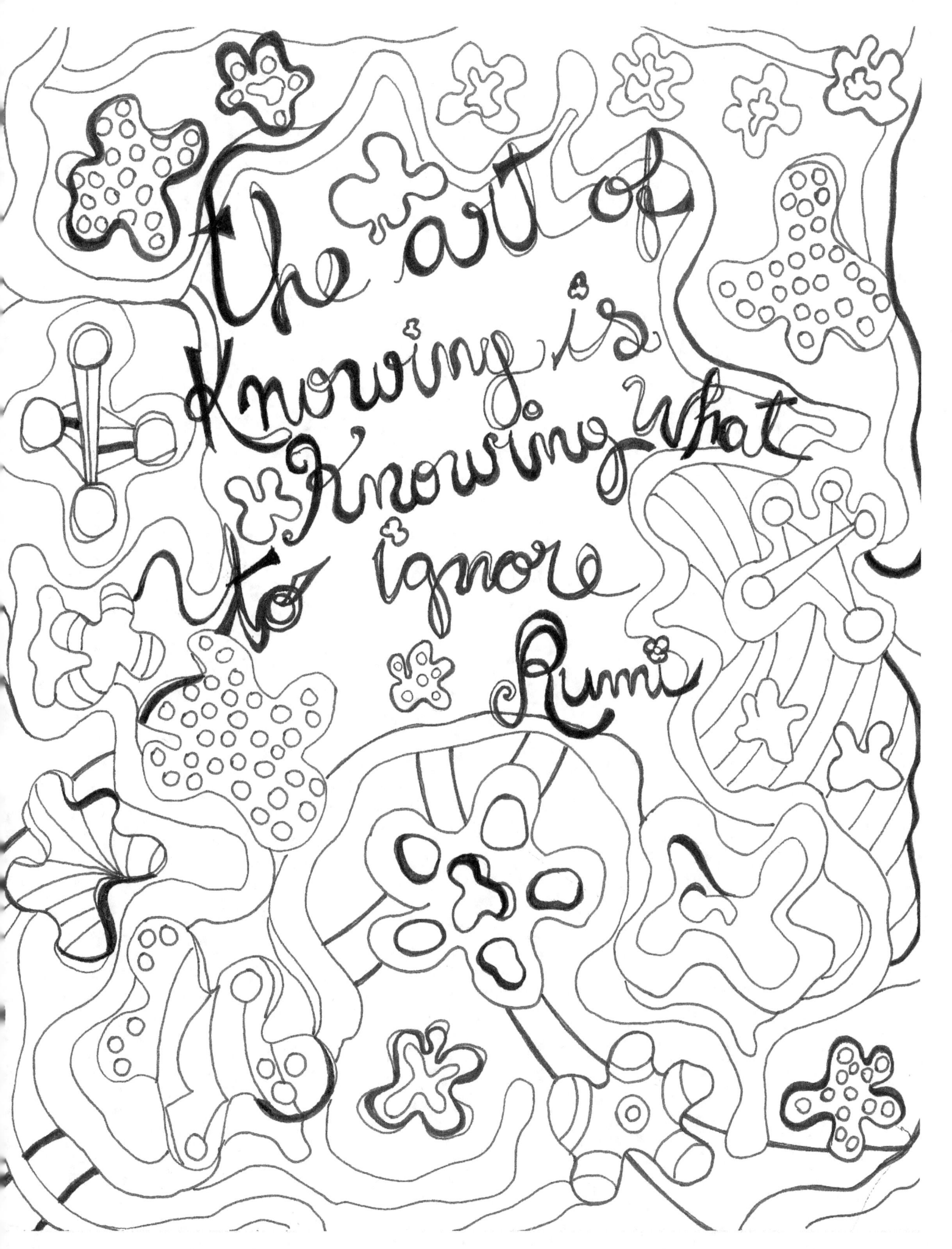

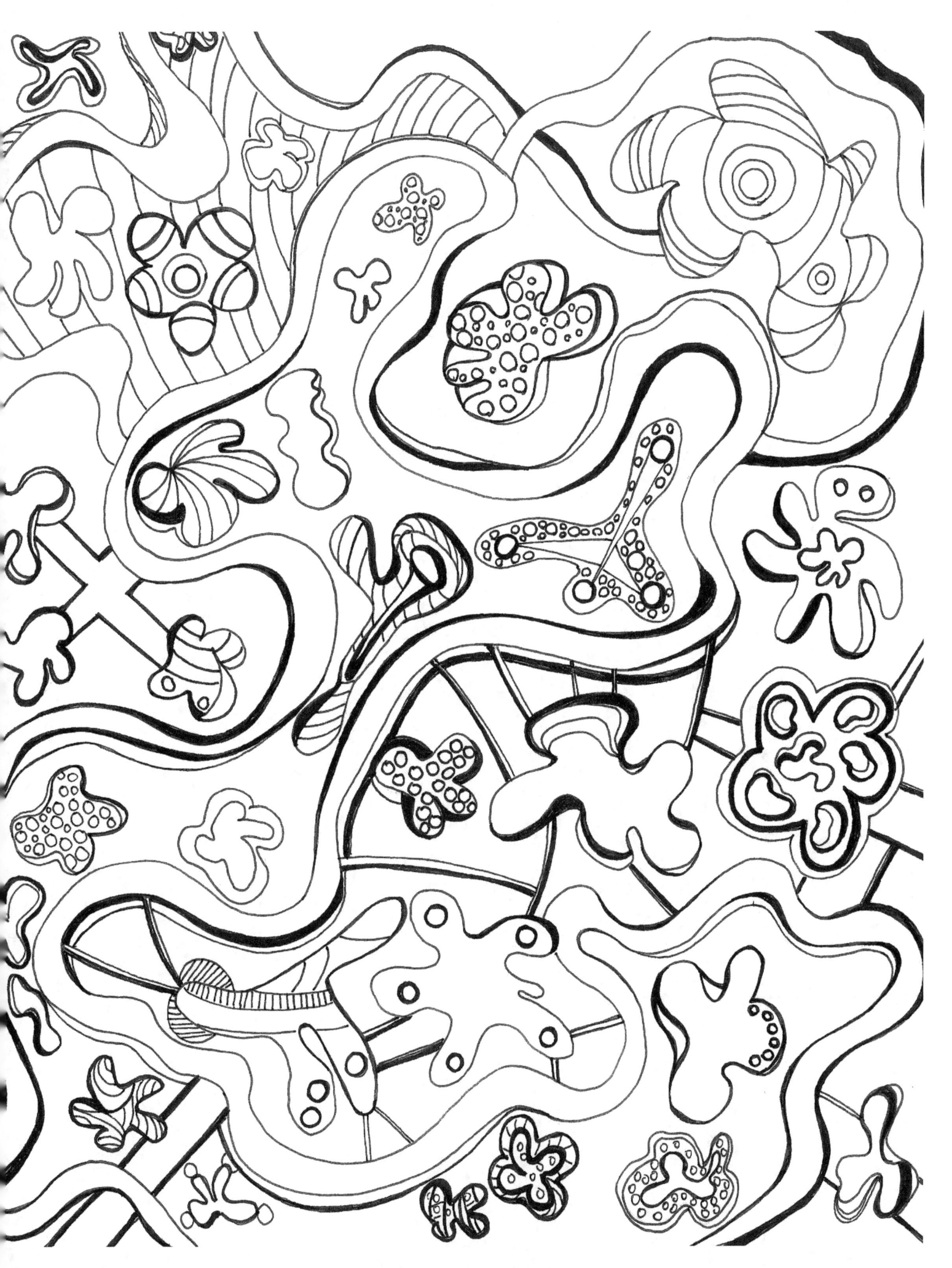

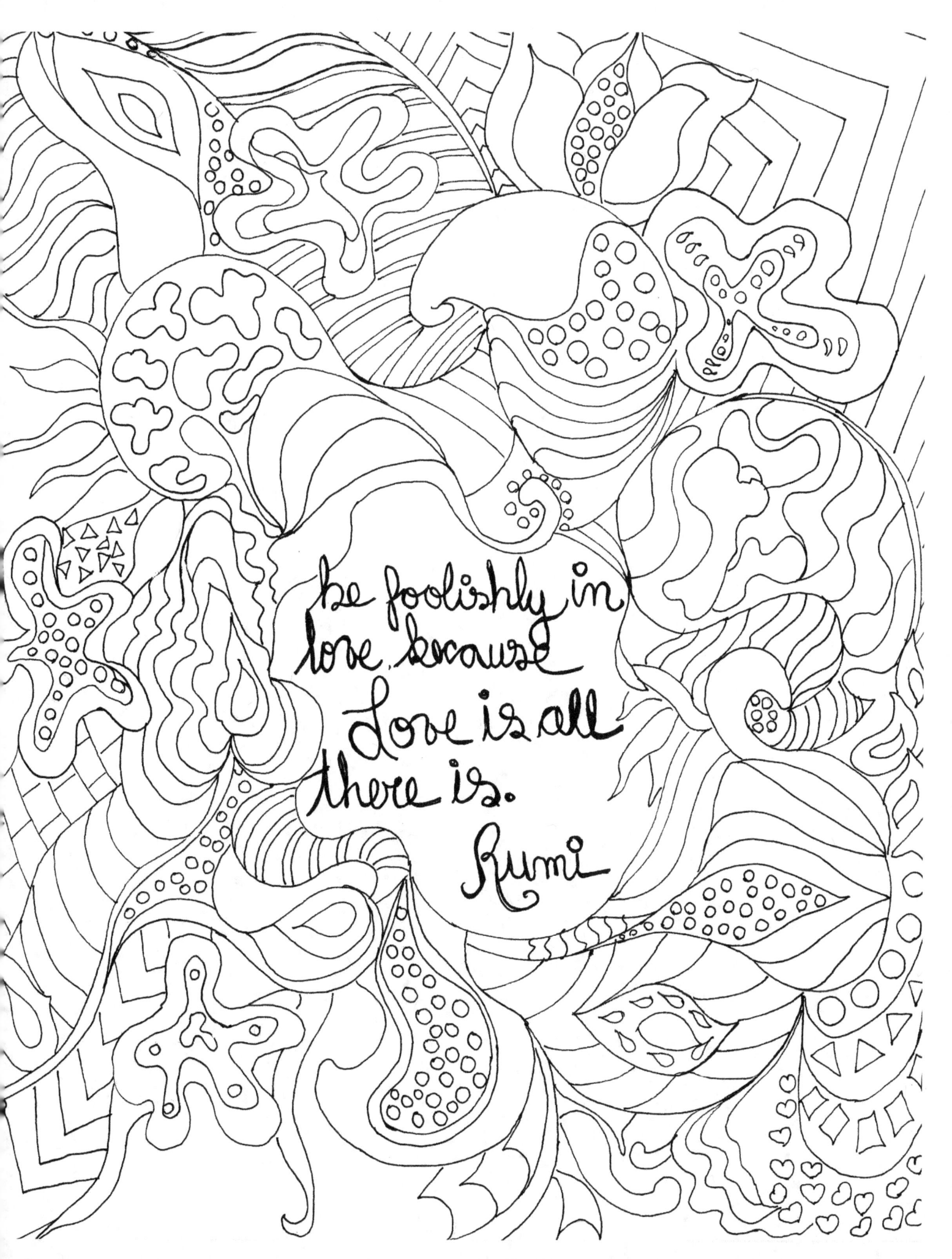

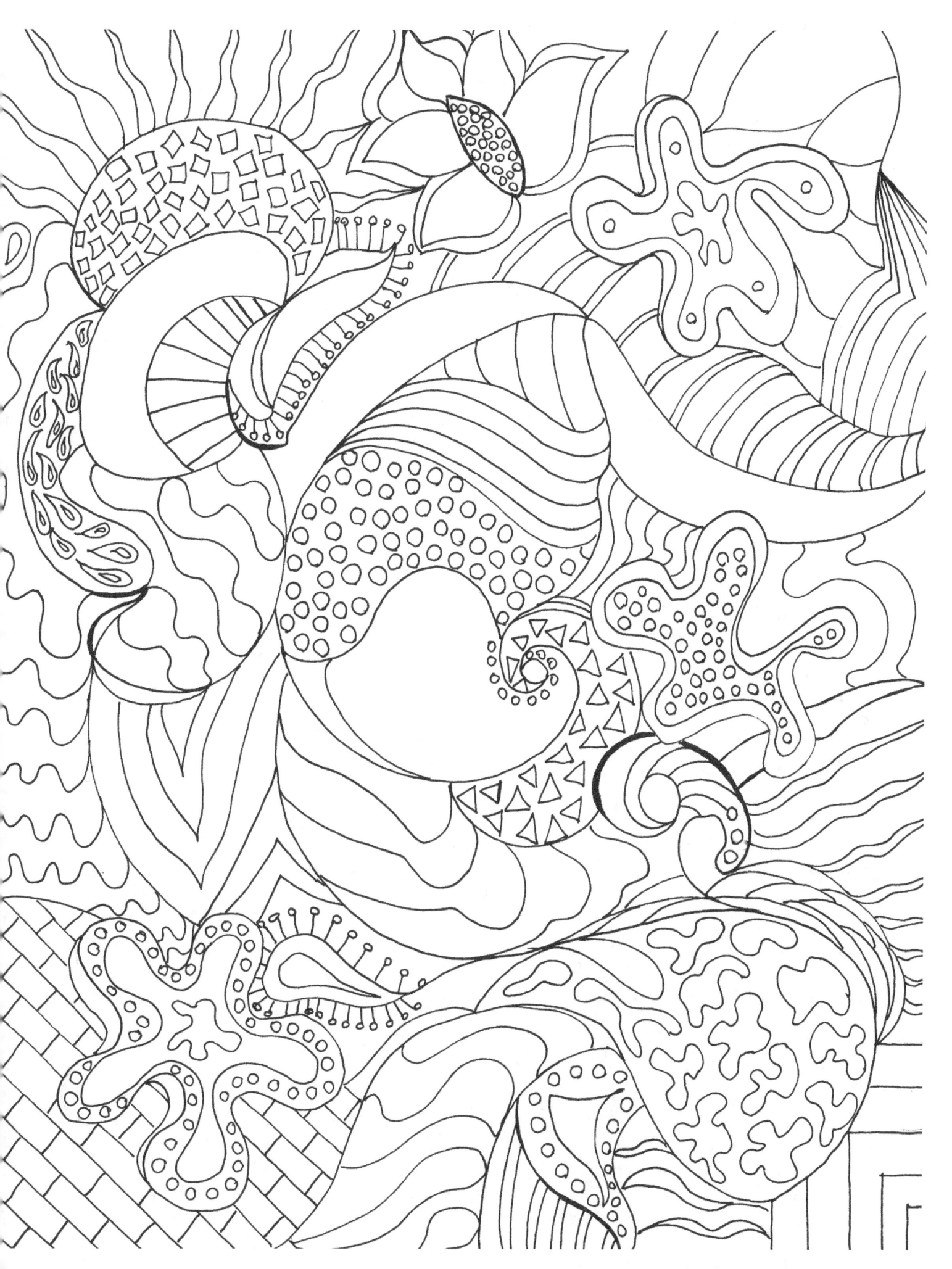

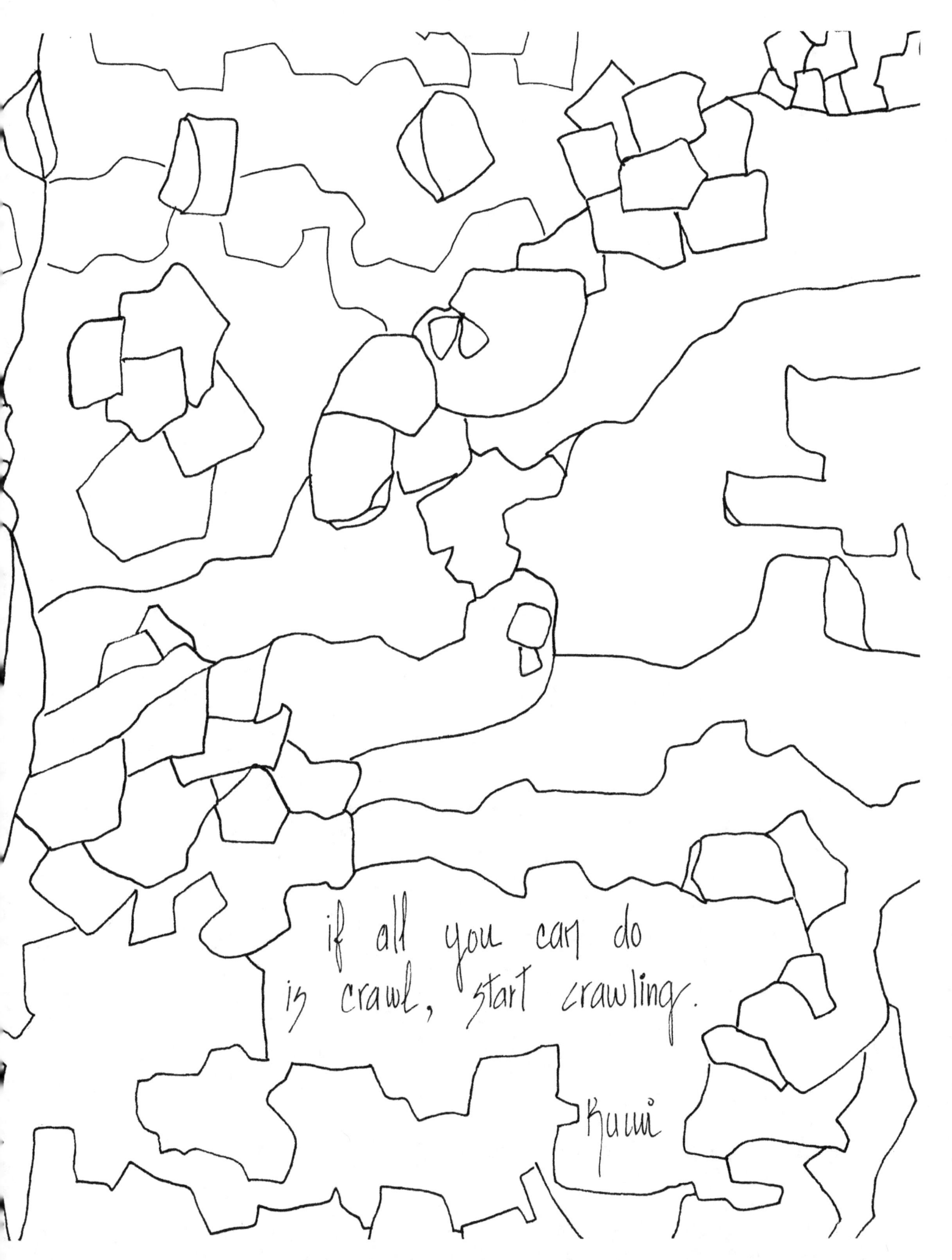

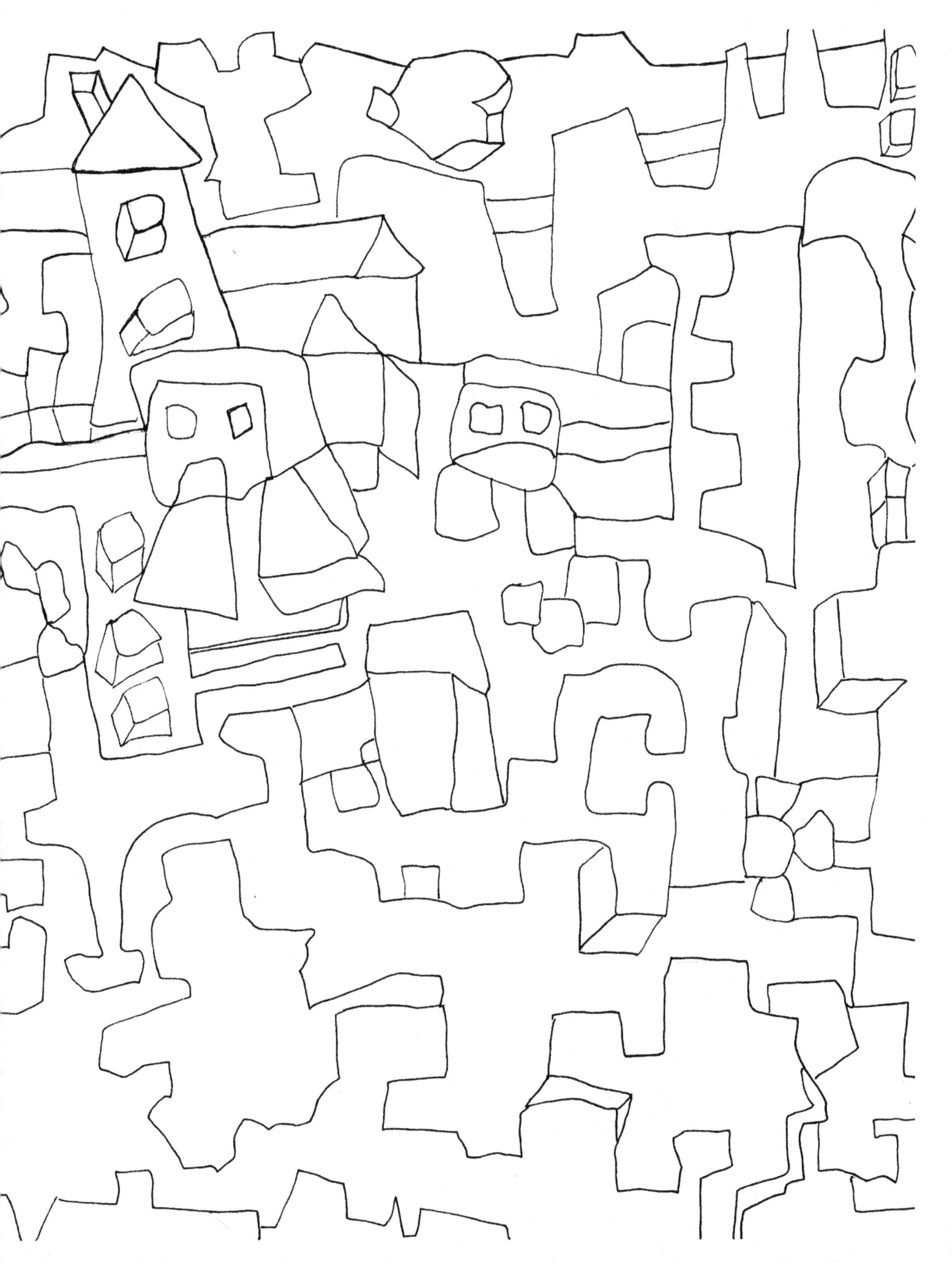

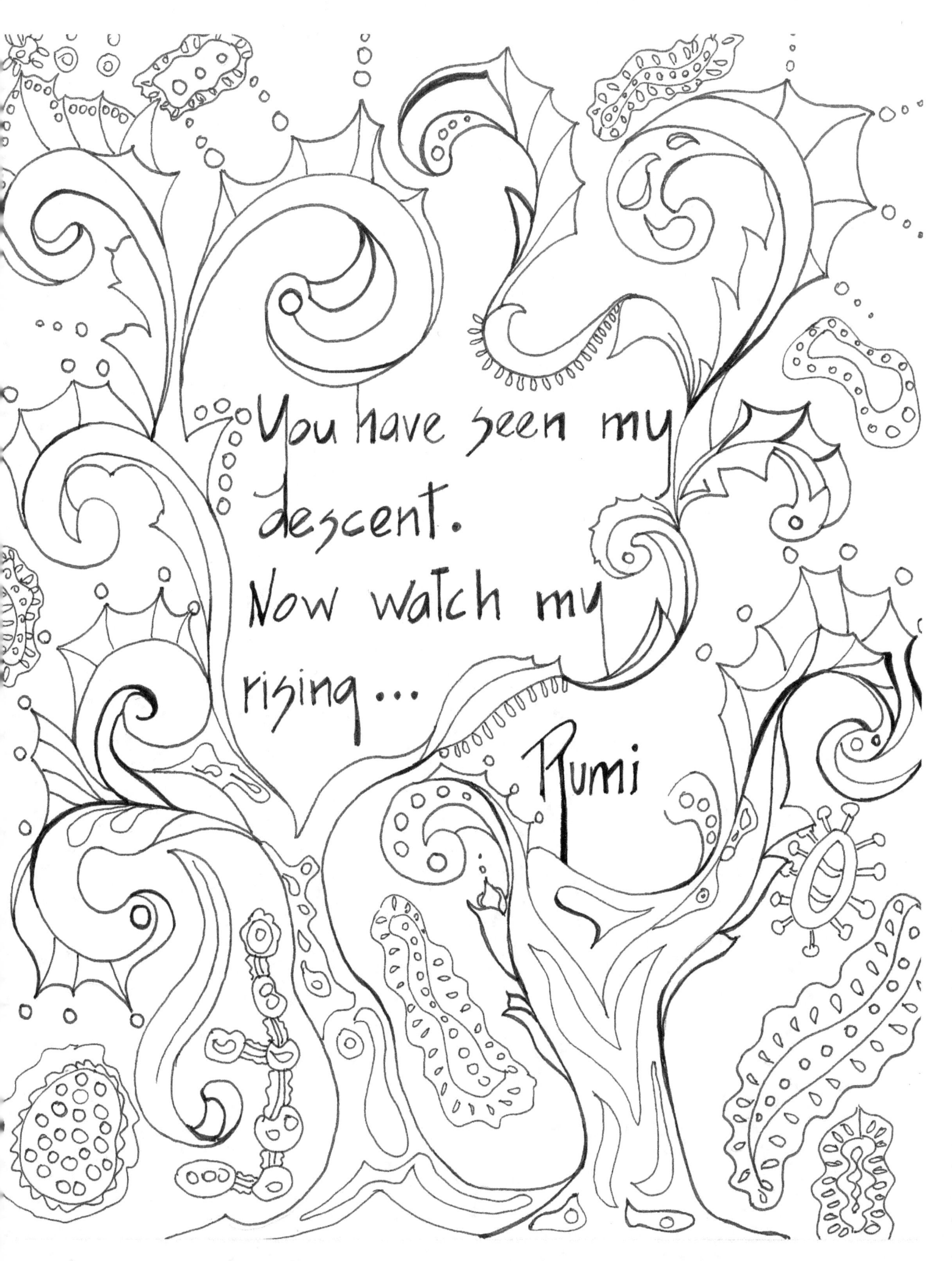

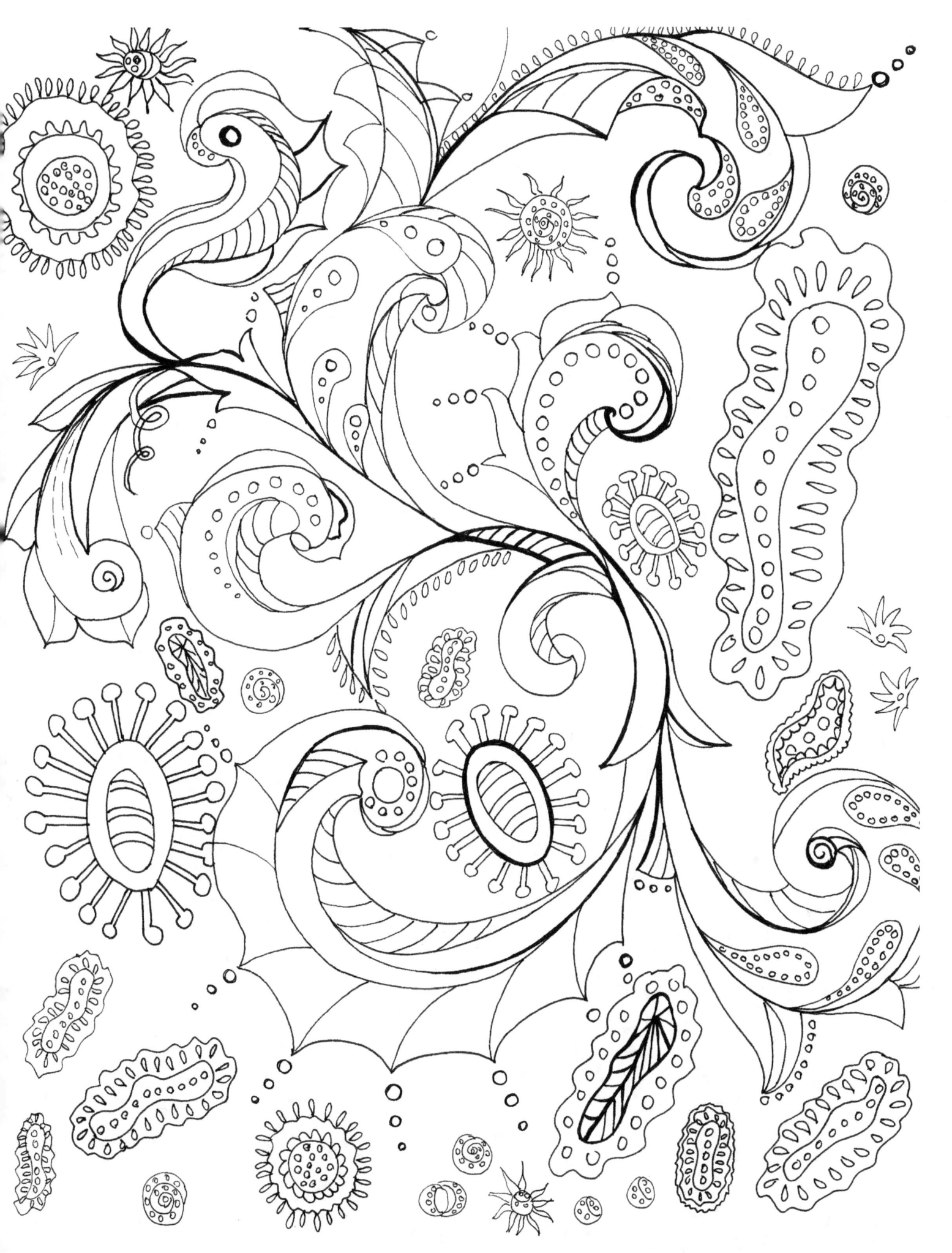

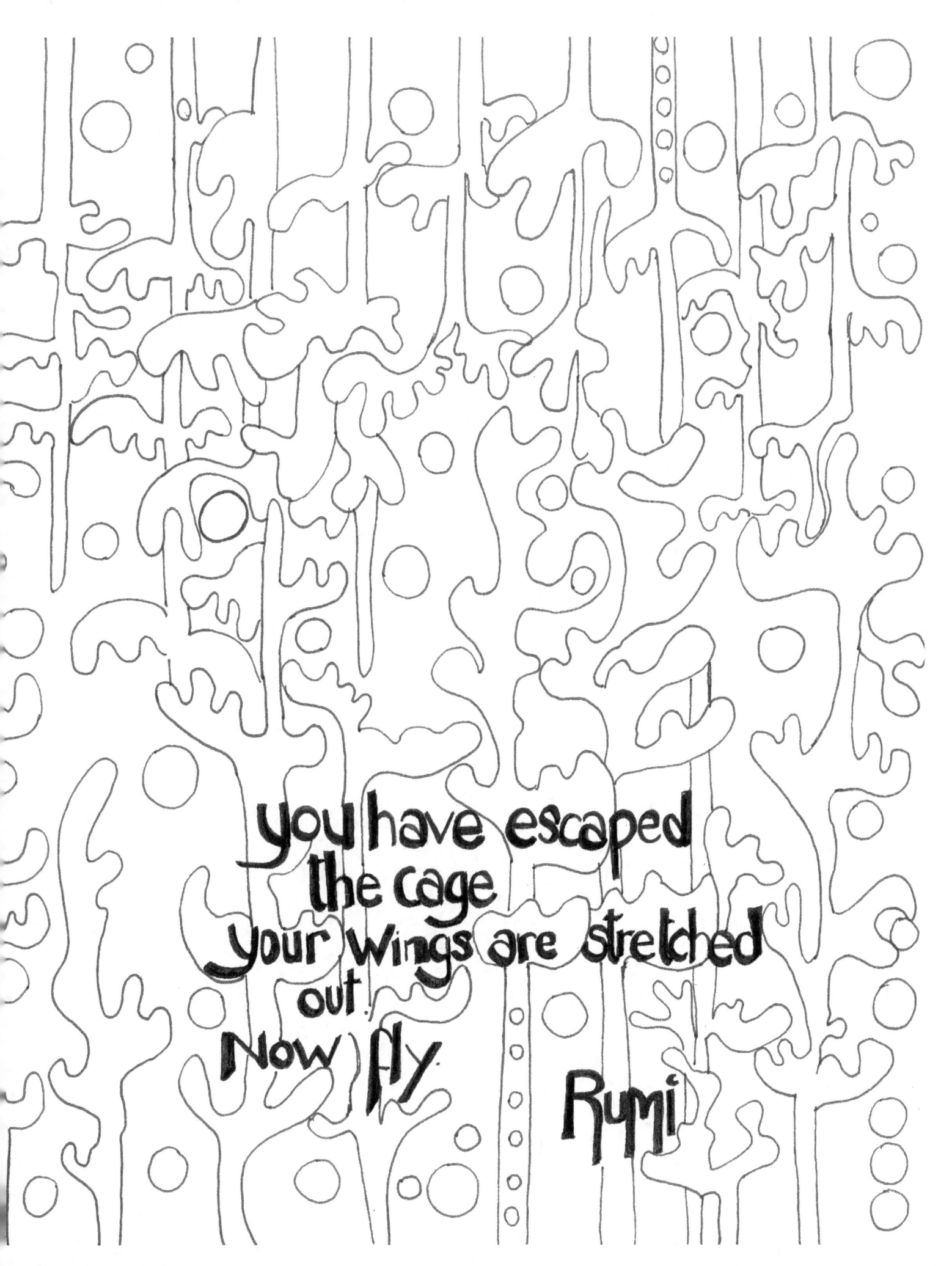

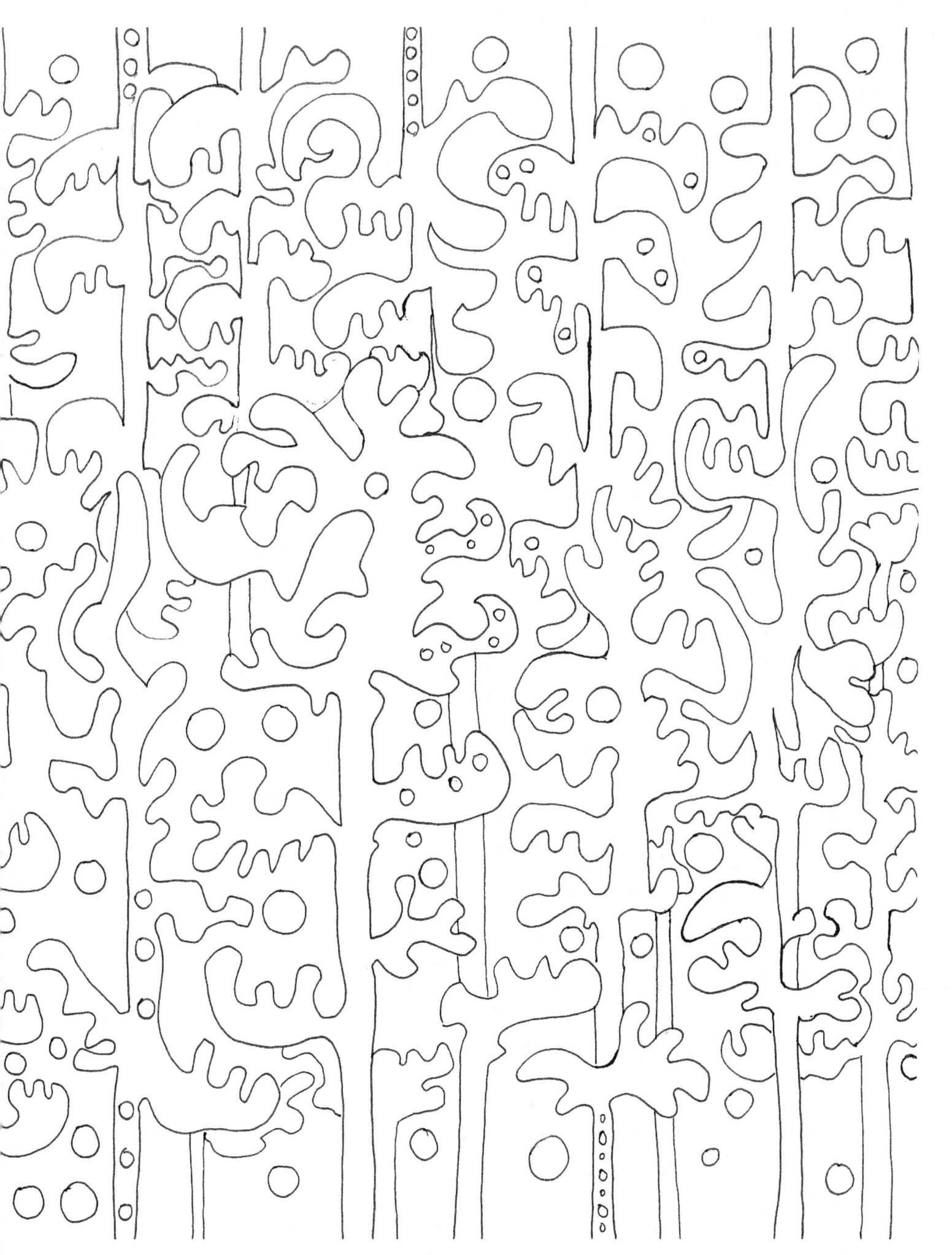

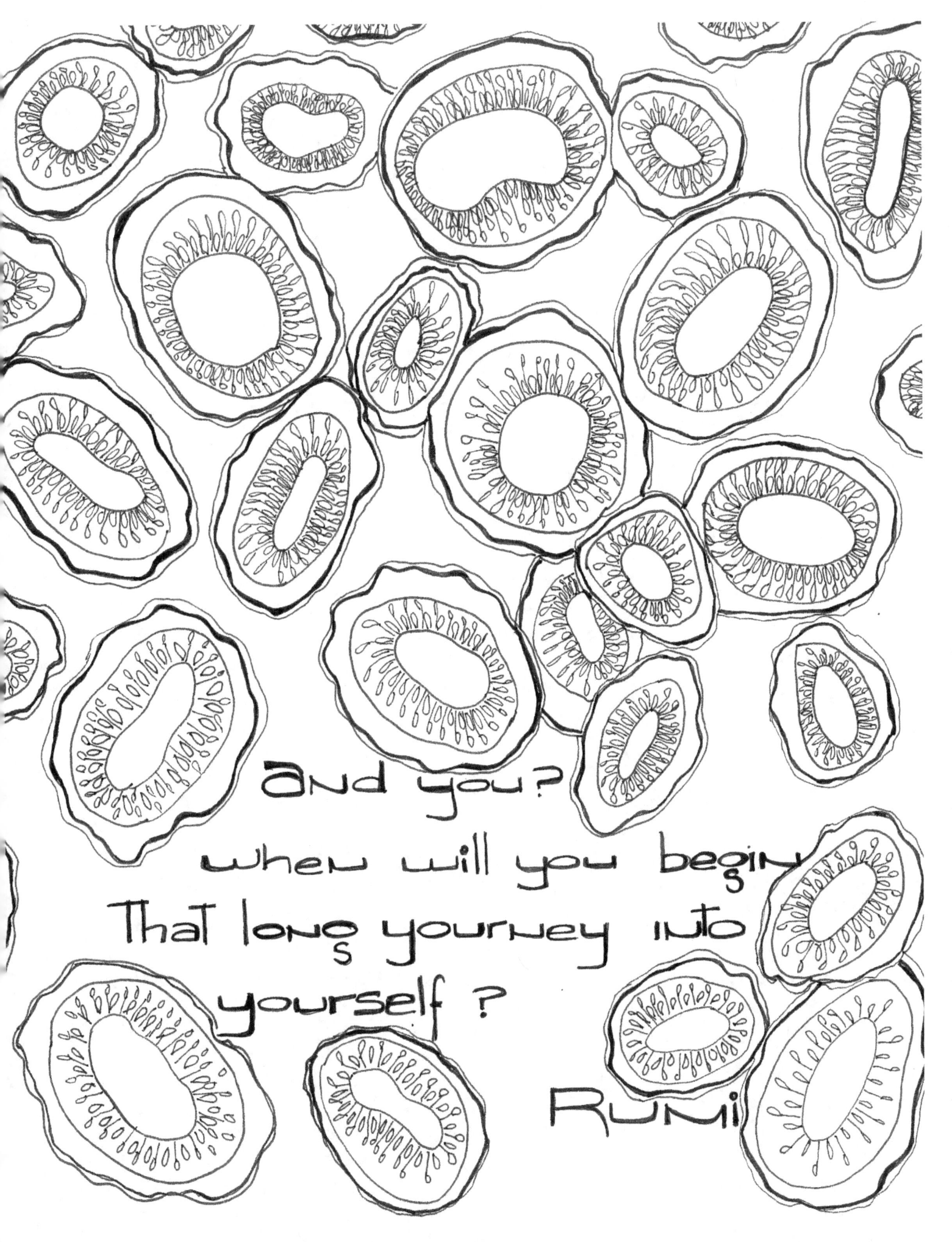

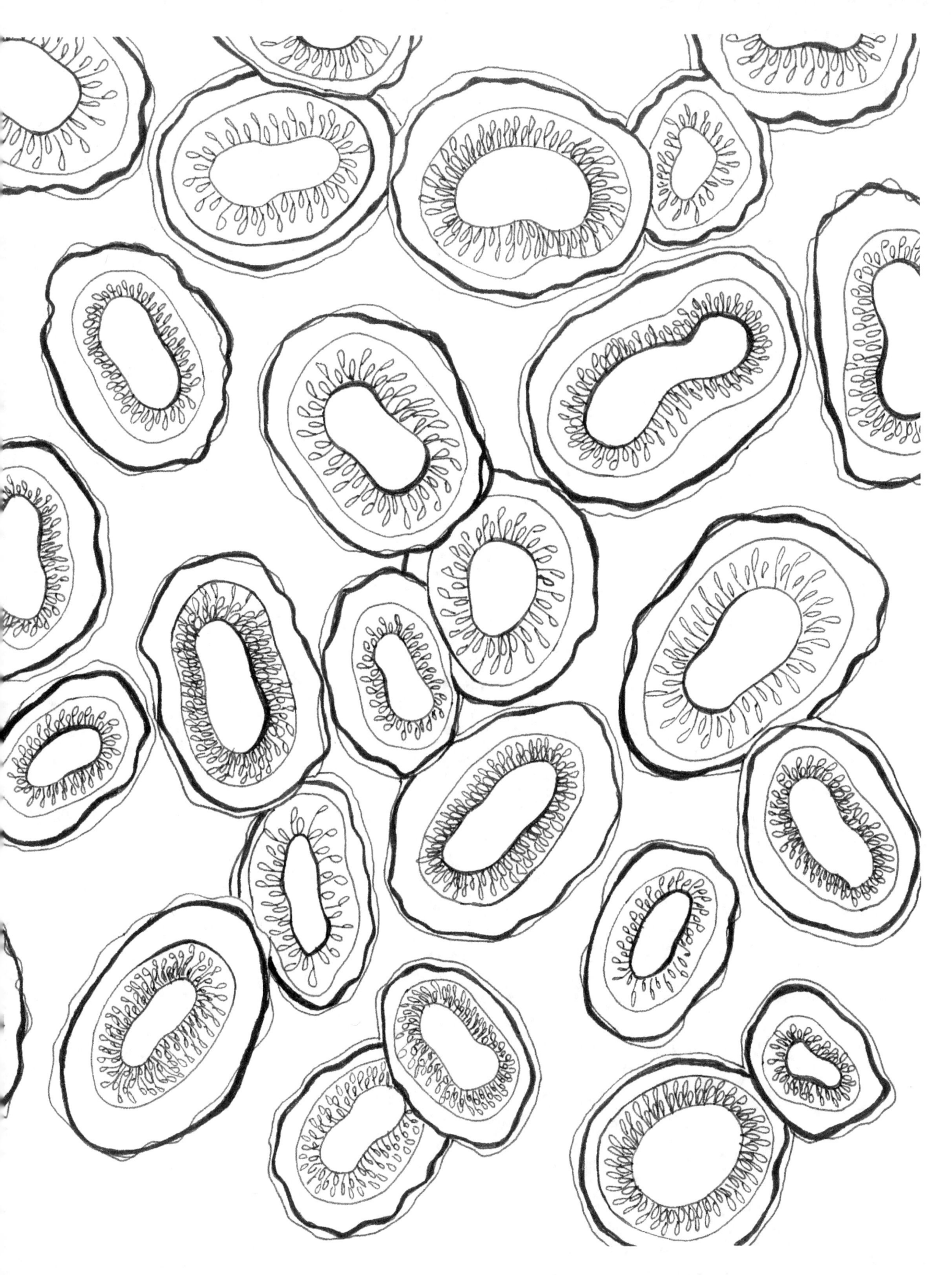

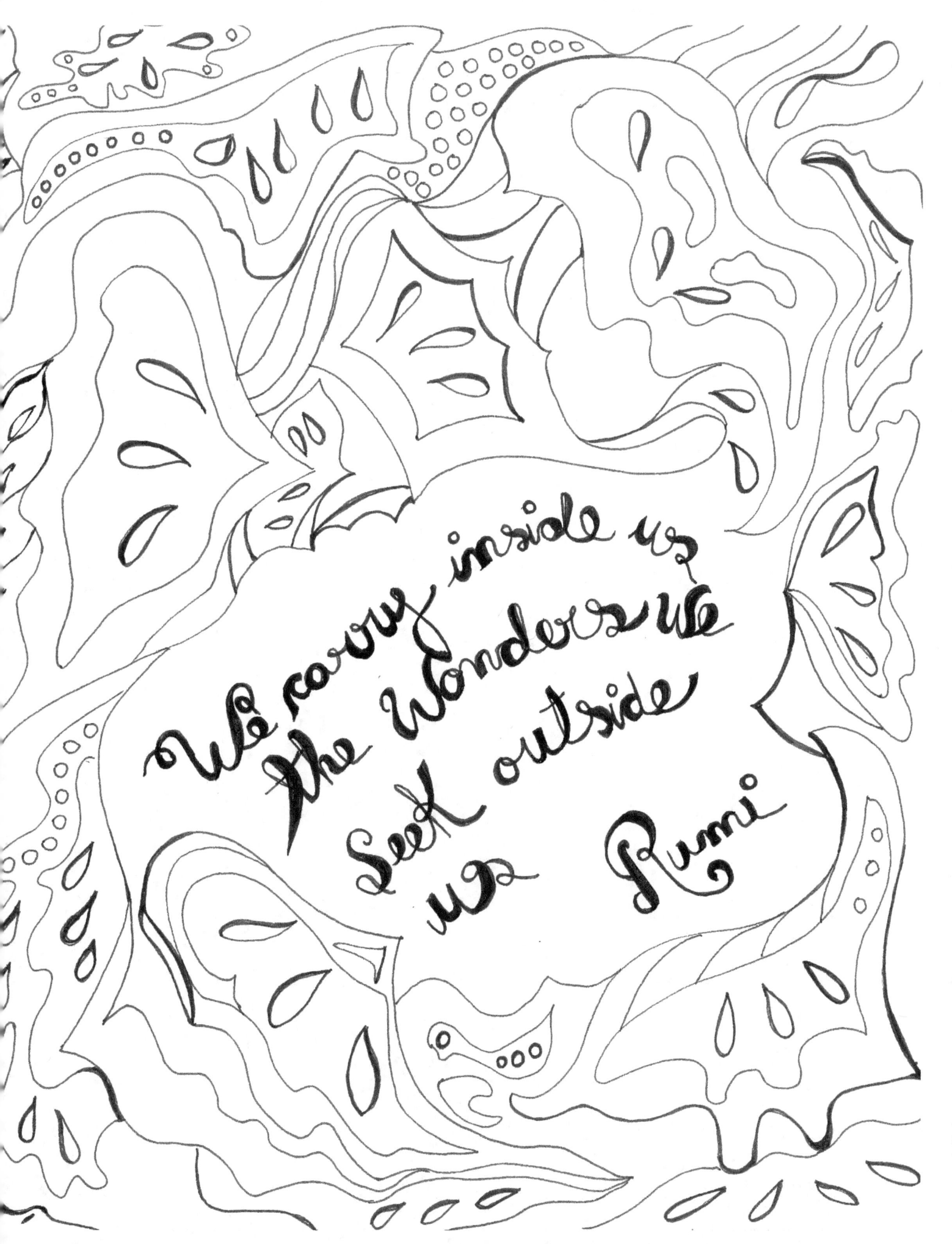

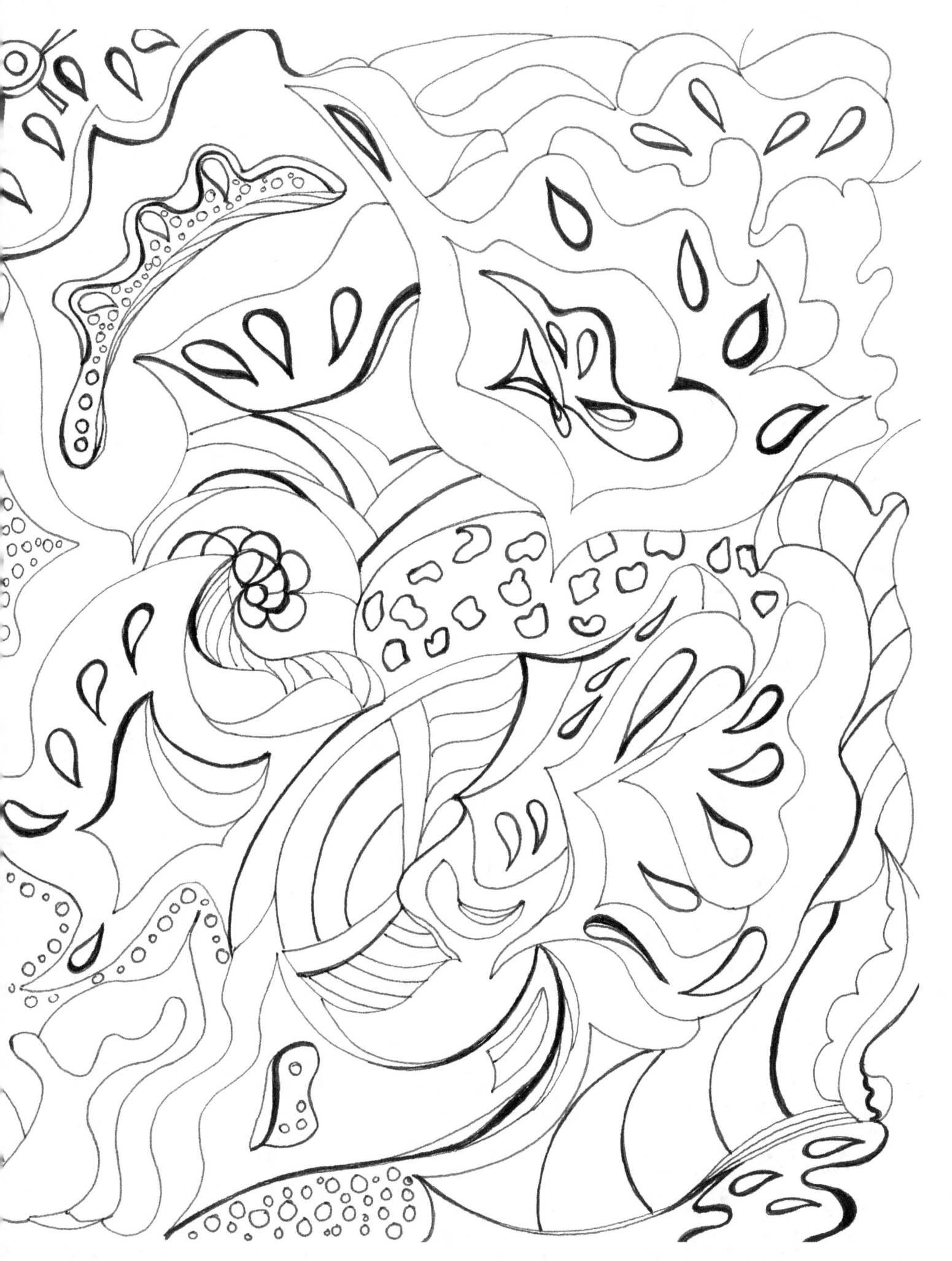

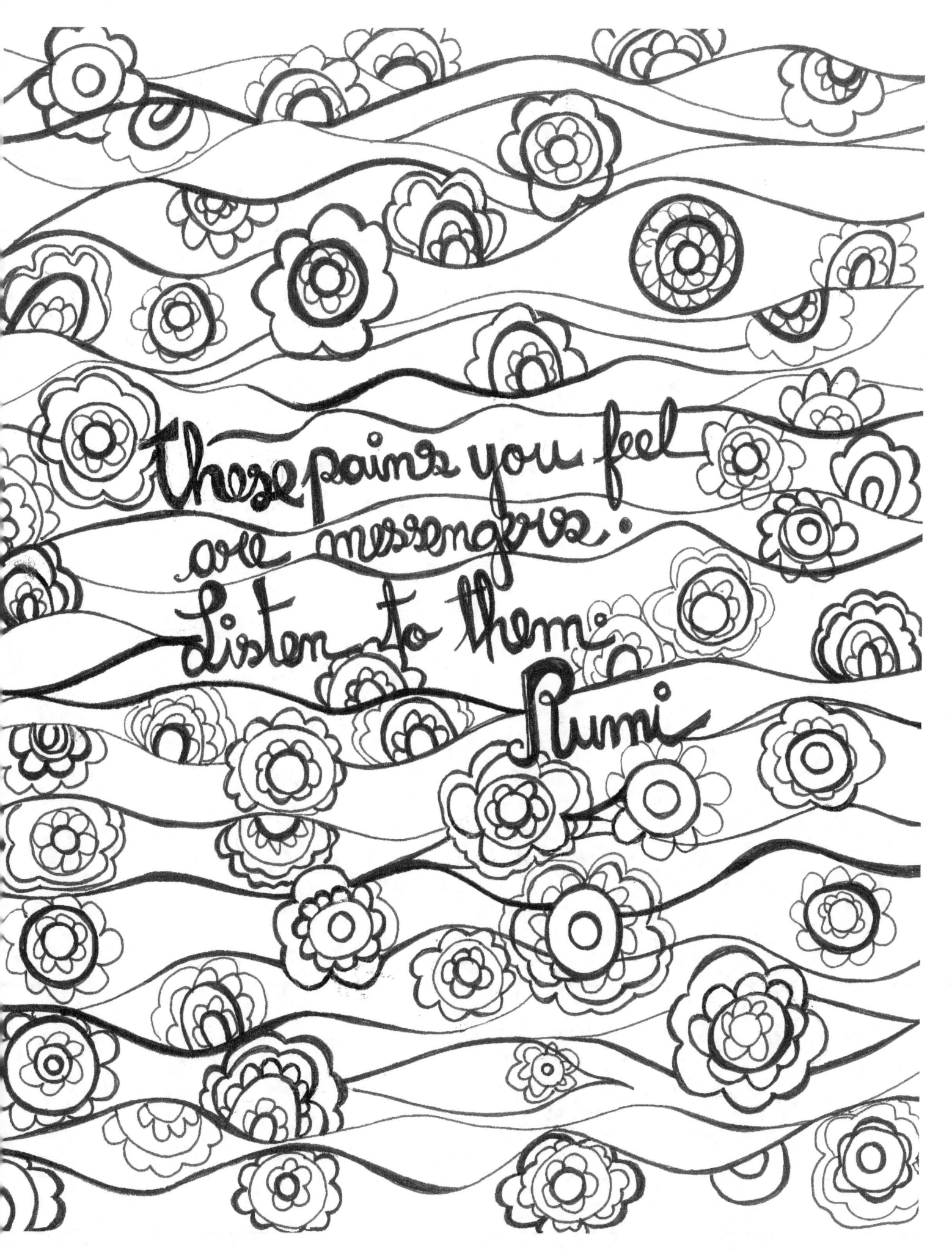

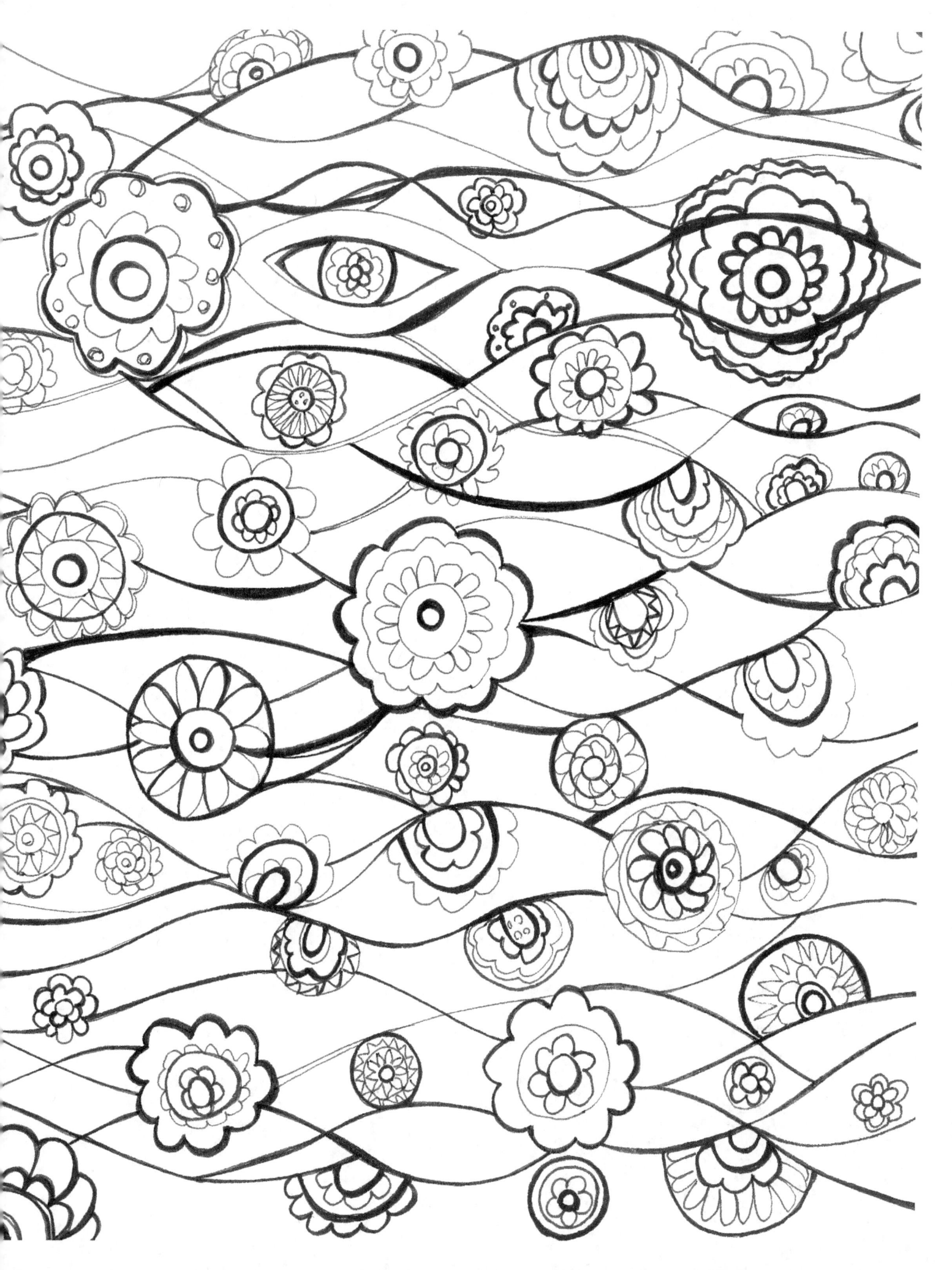

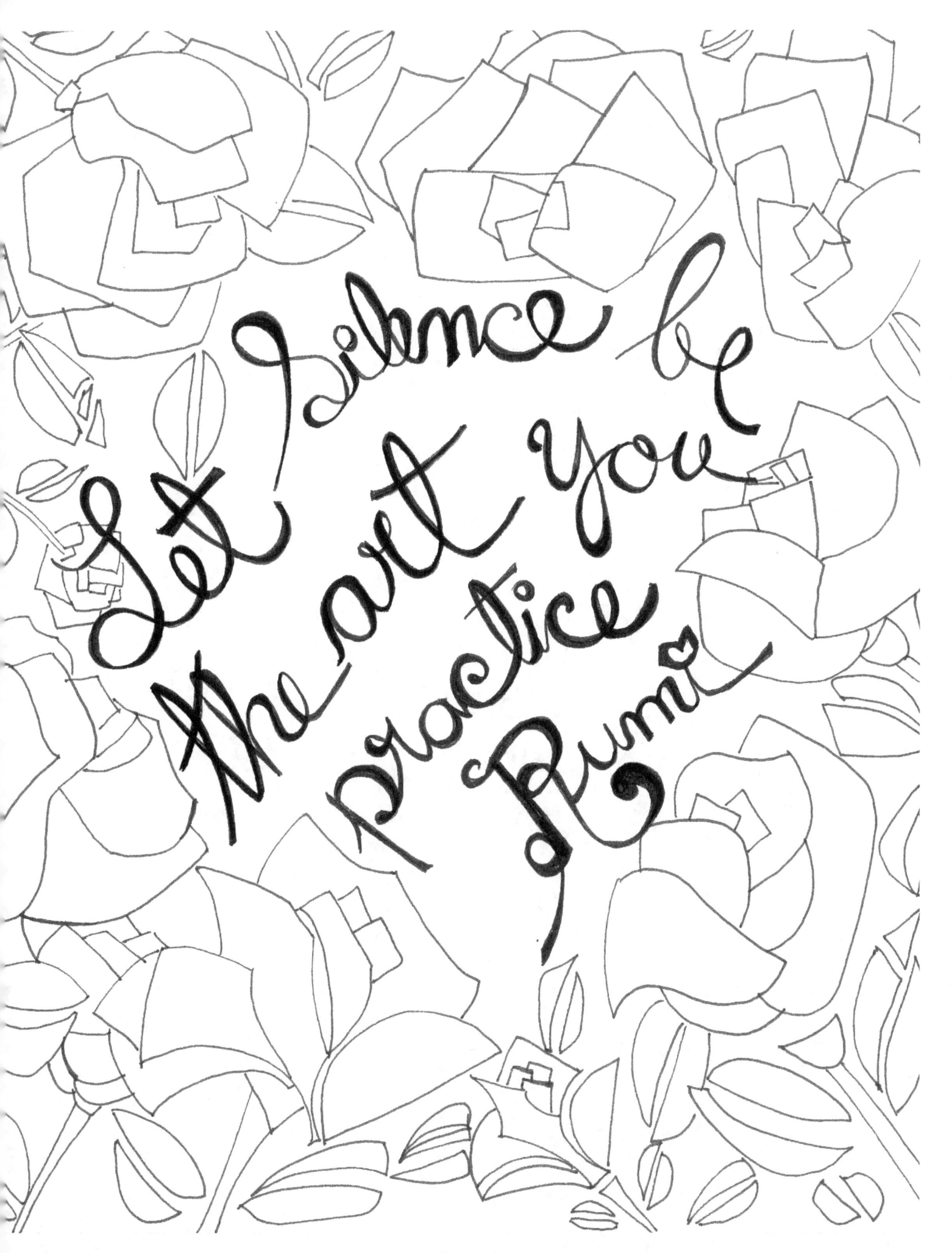

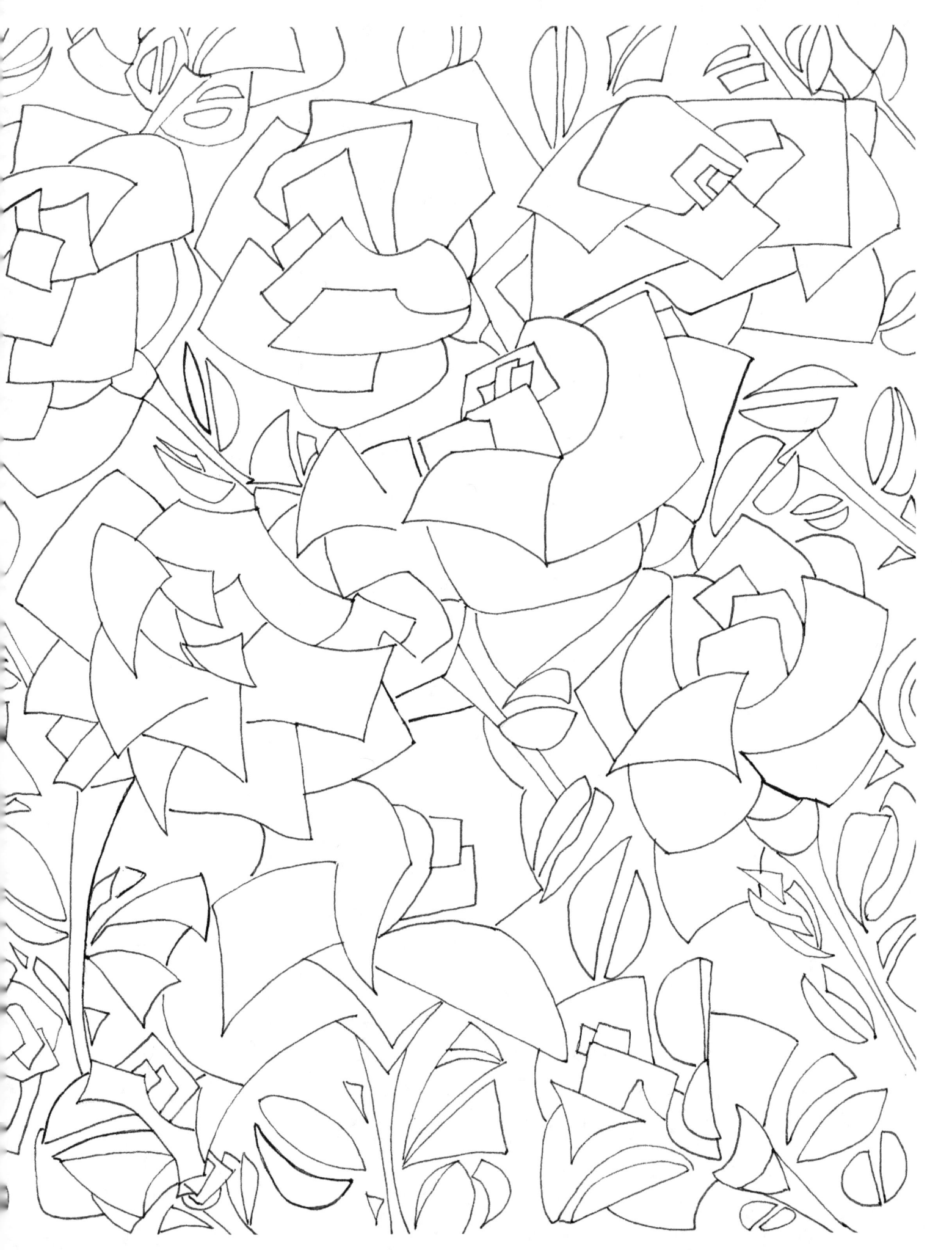

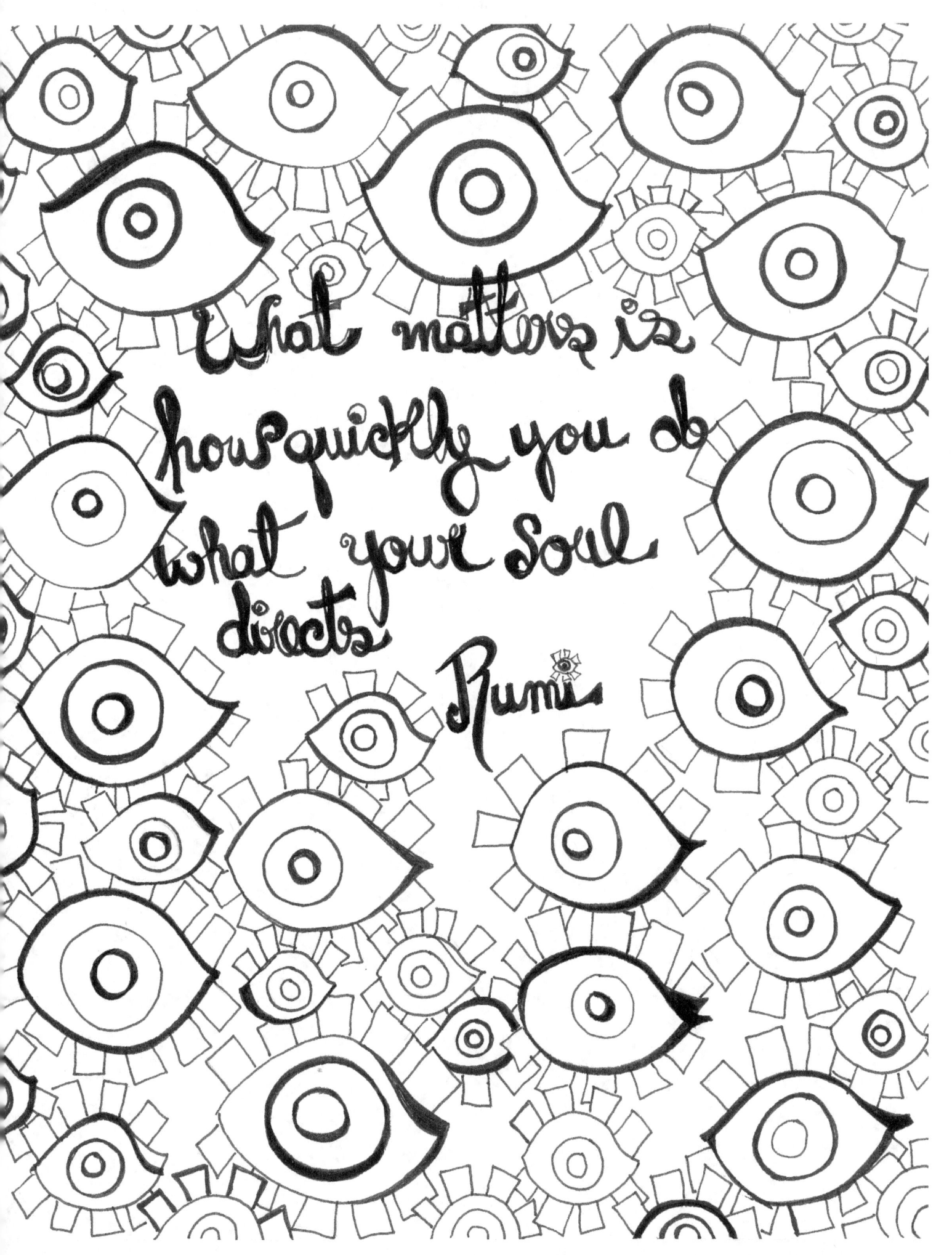

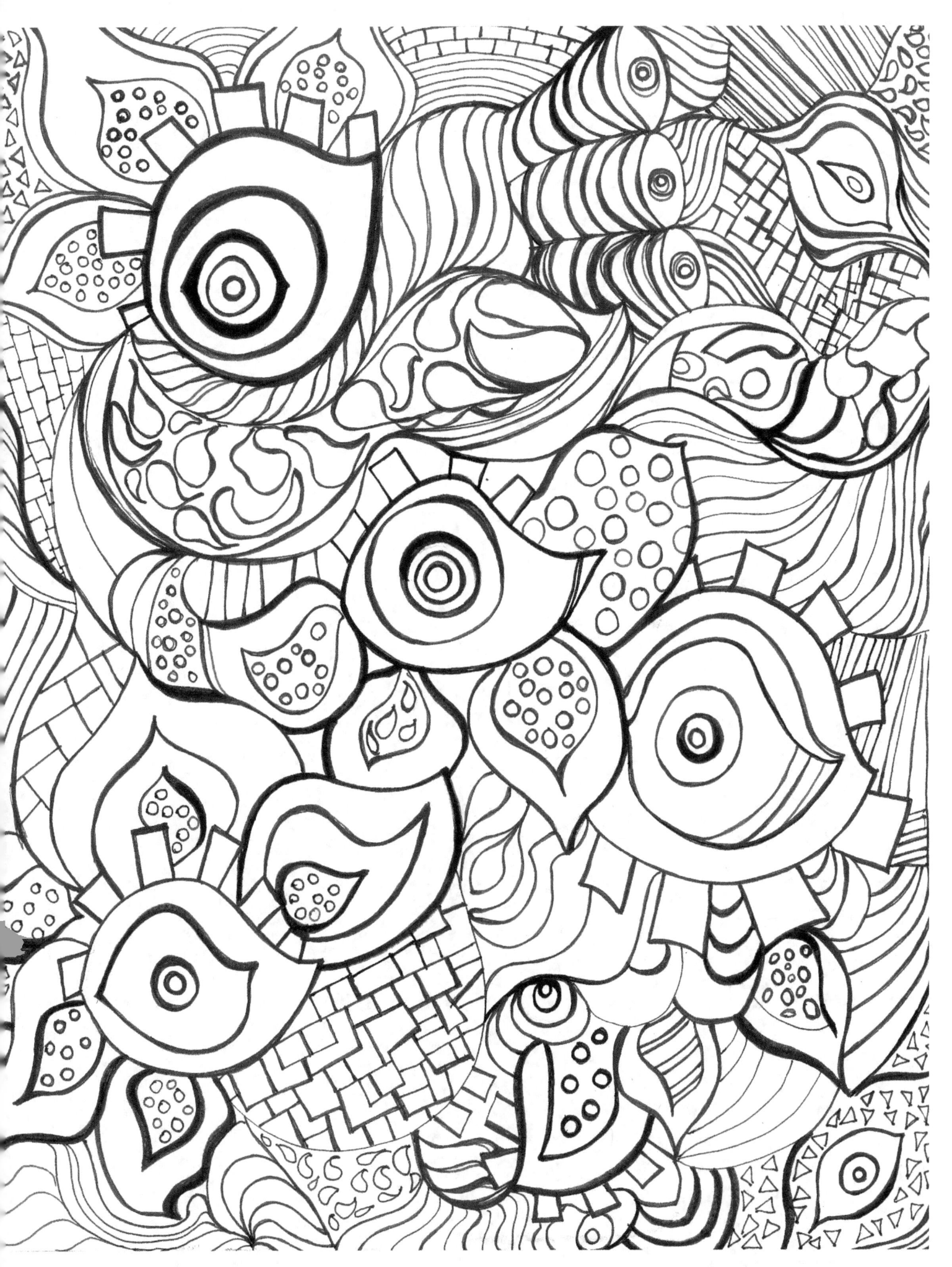

Your task is not to seek for love, but merely to seek and find all the barriers within yourself that you have built against it
Rumi

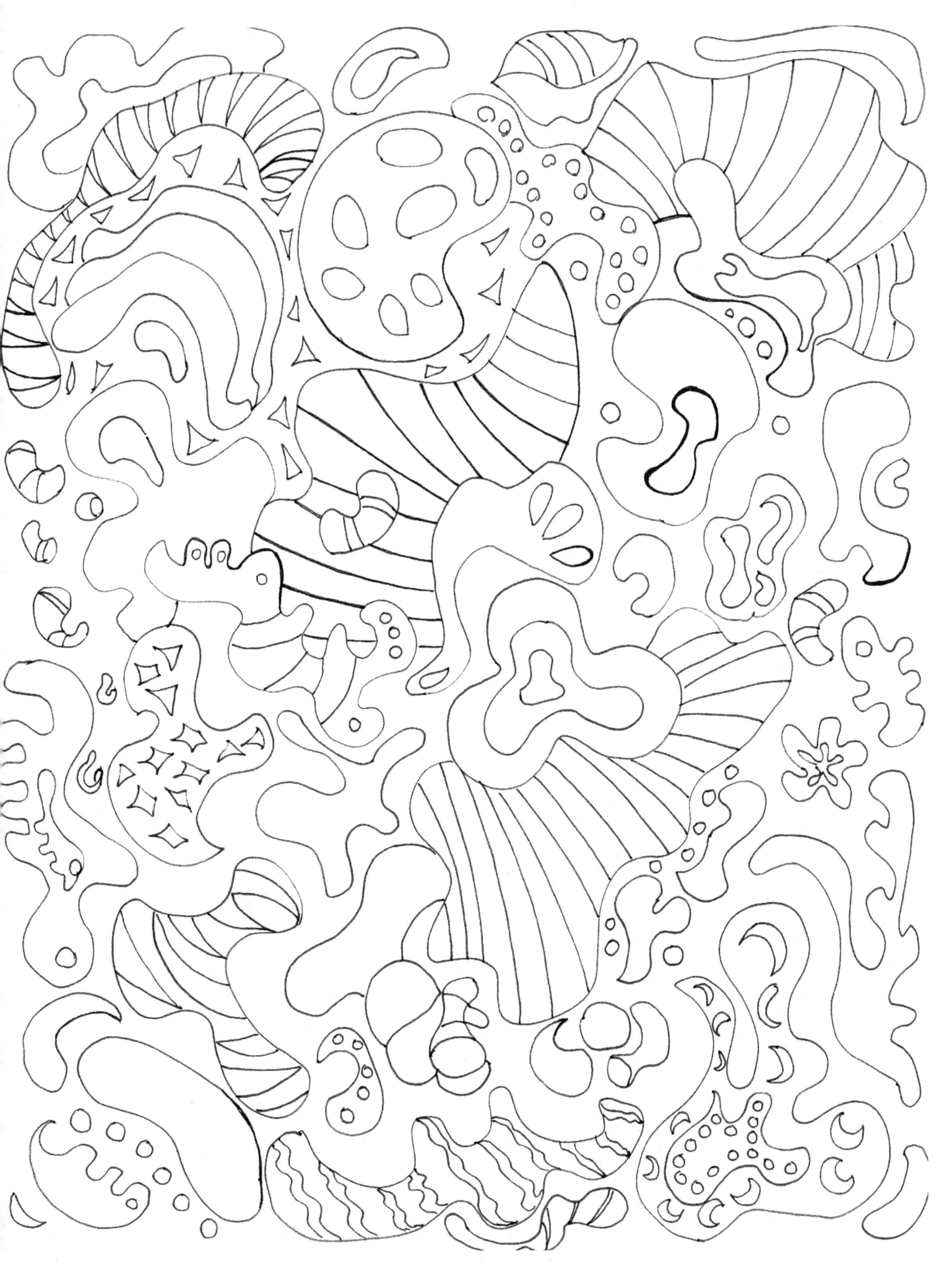

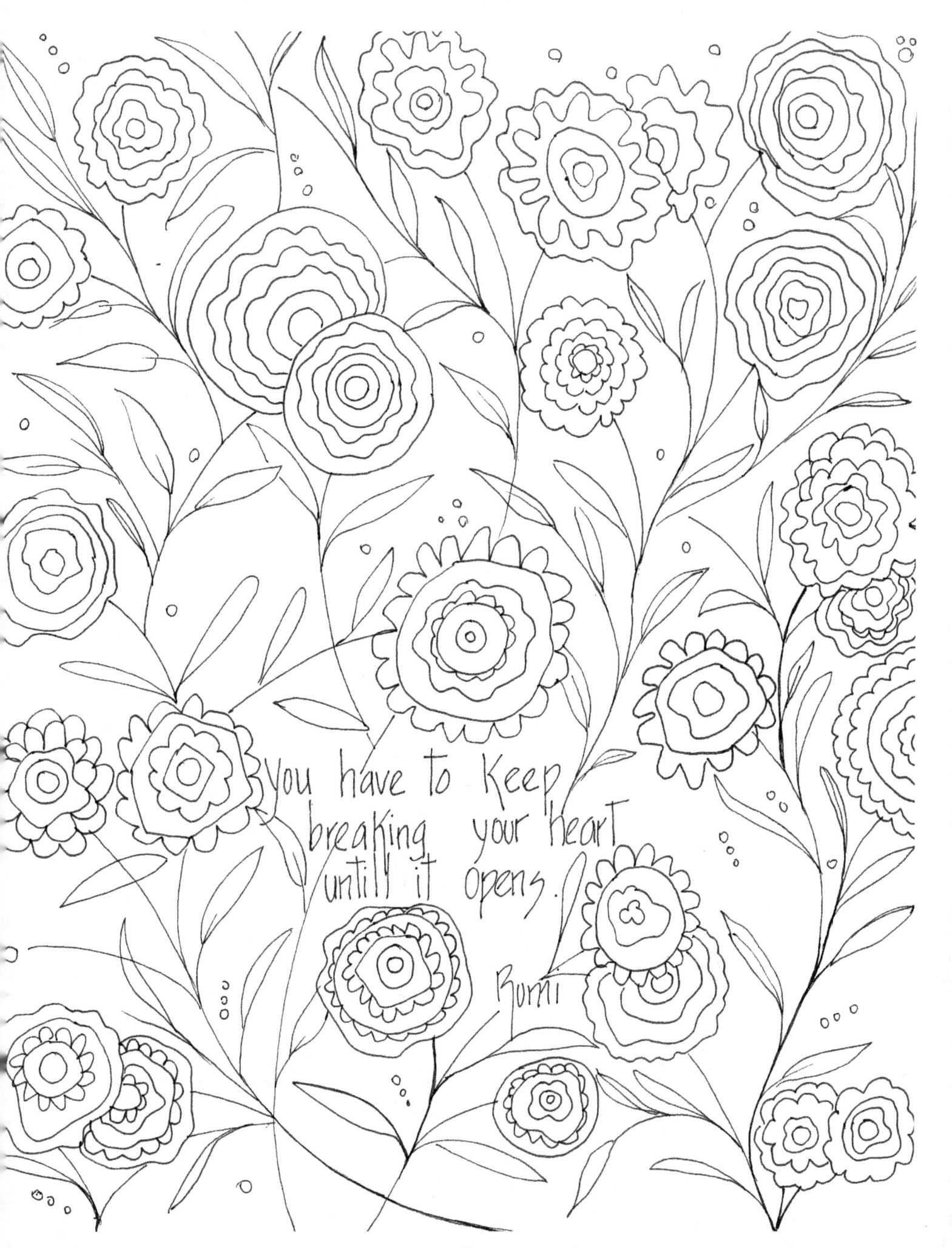

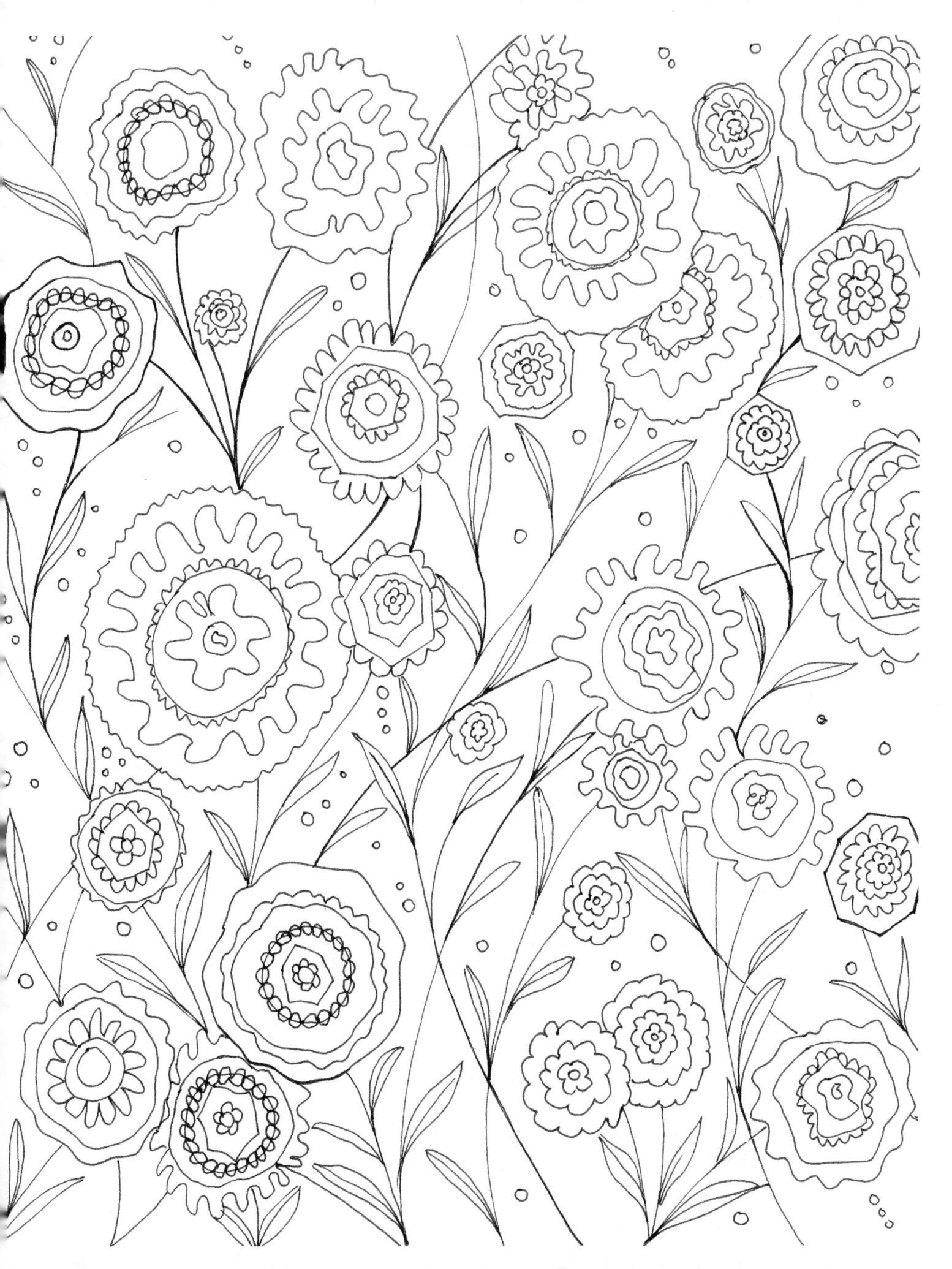

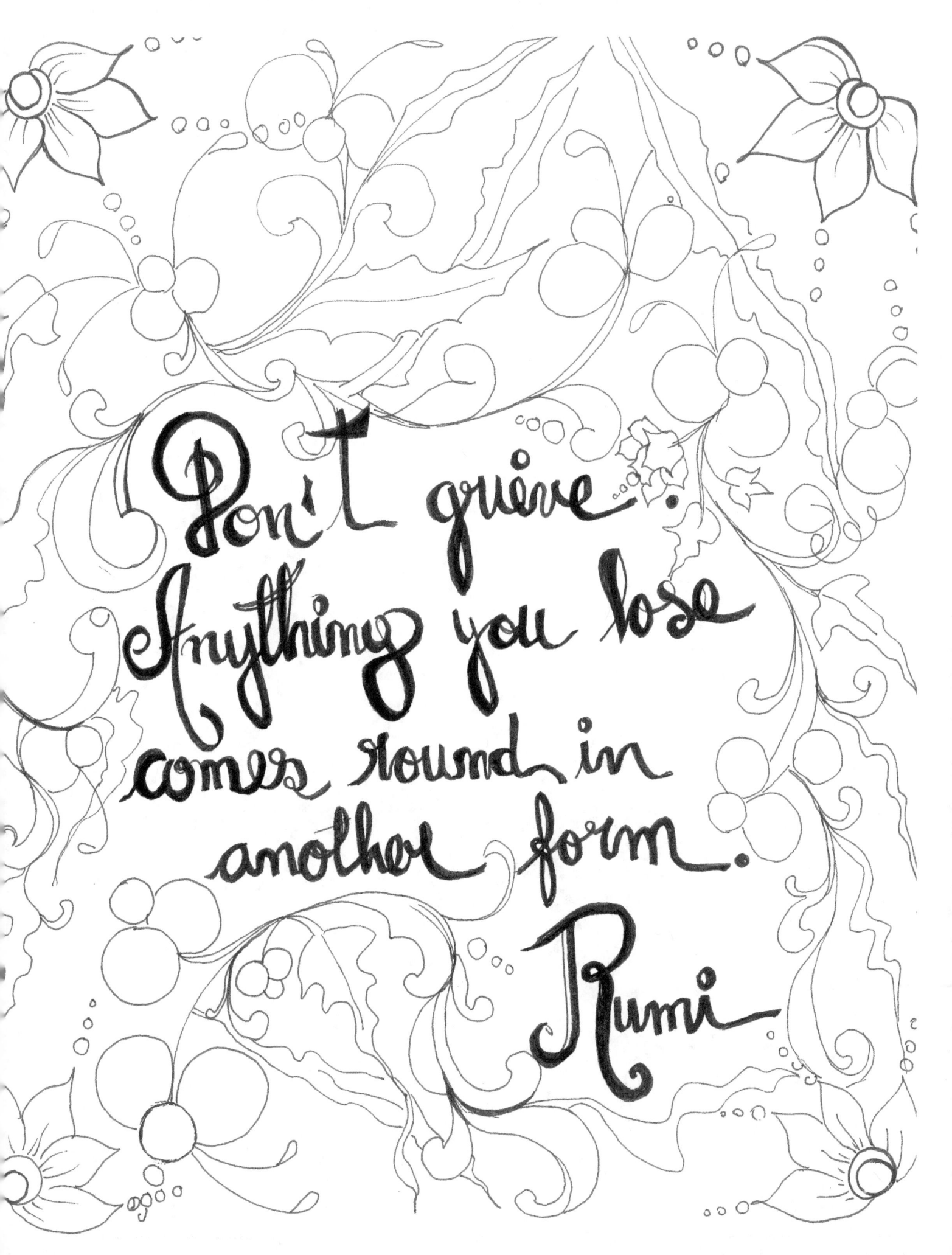

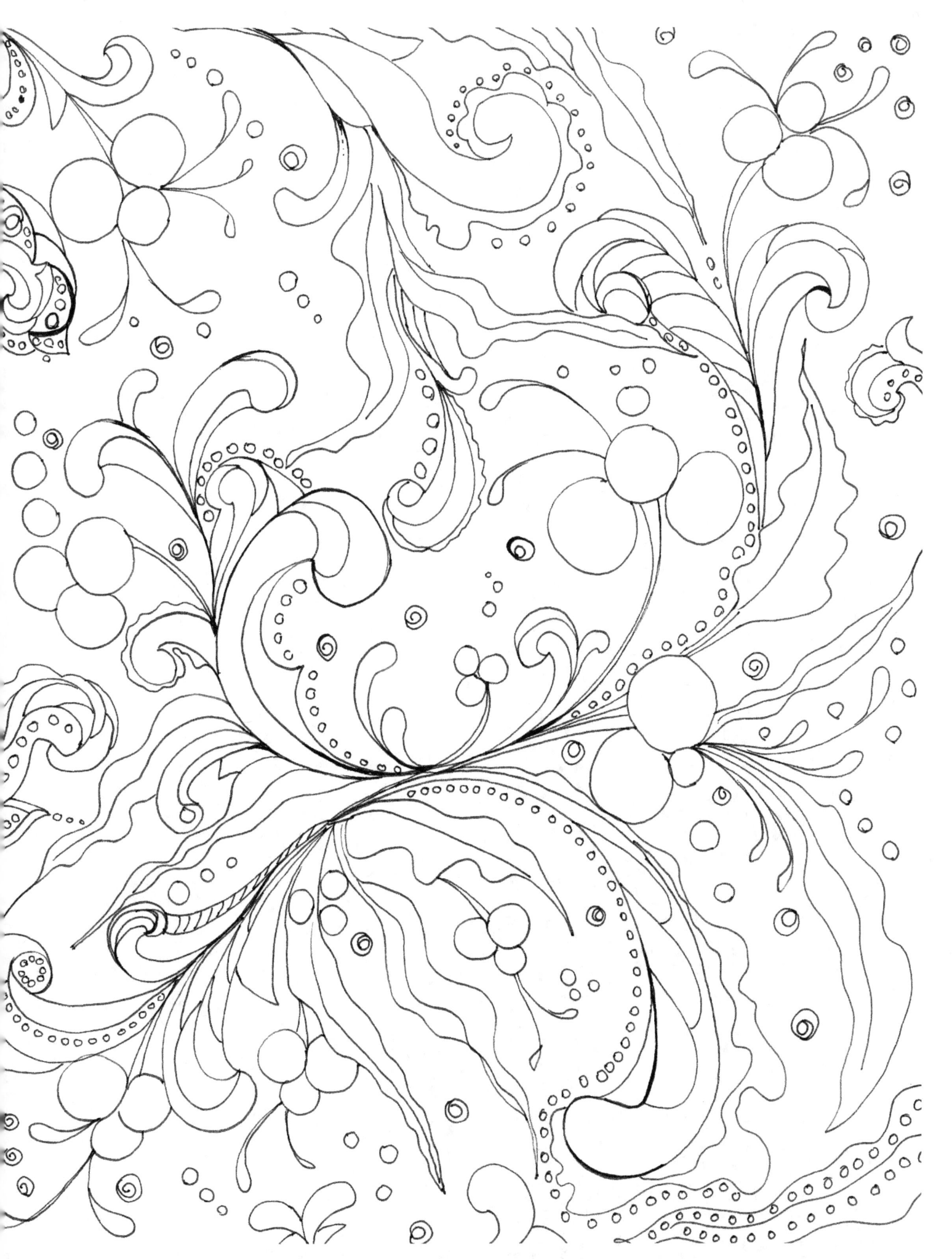

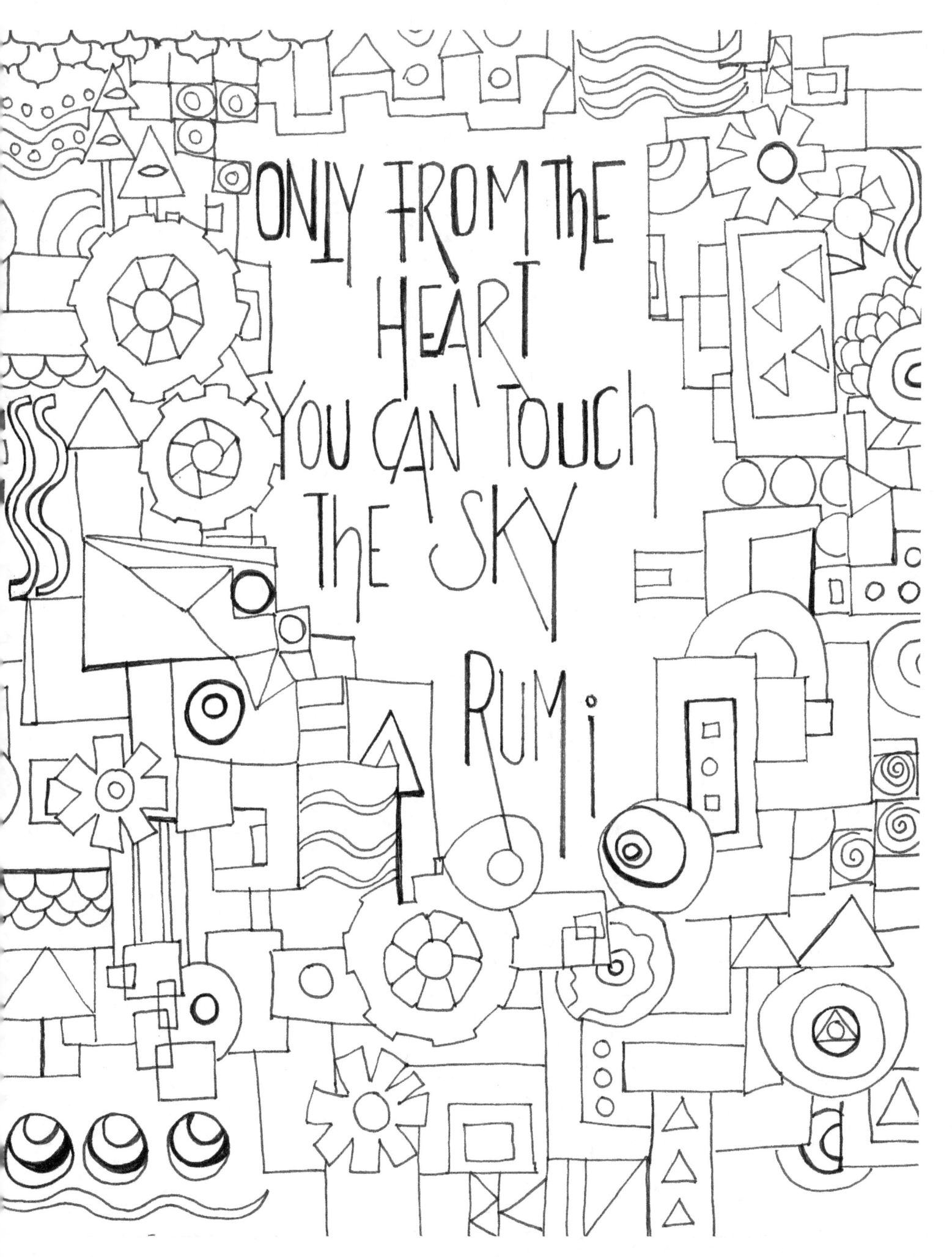

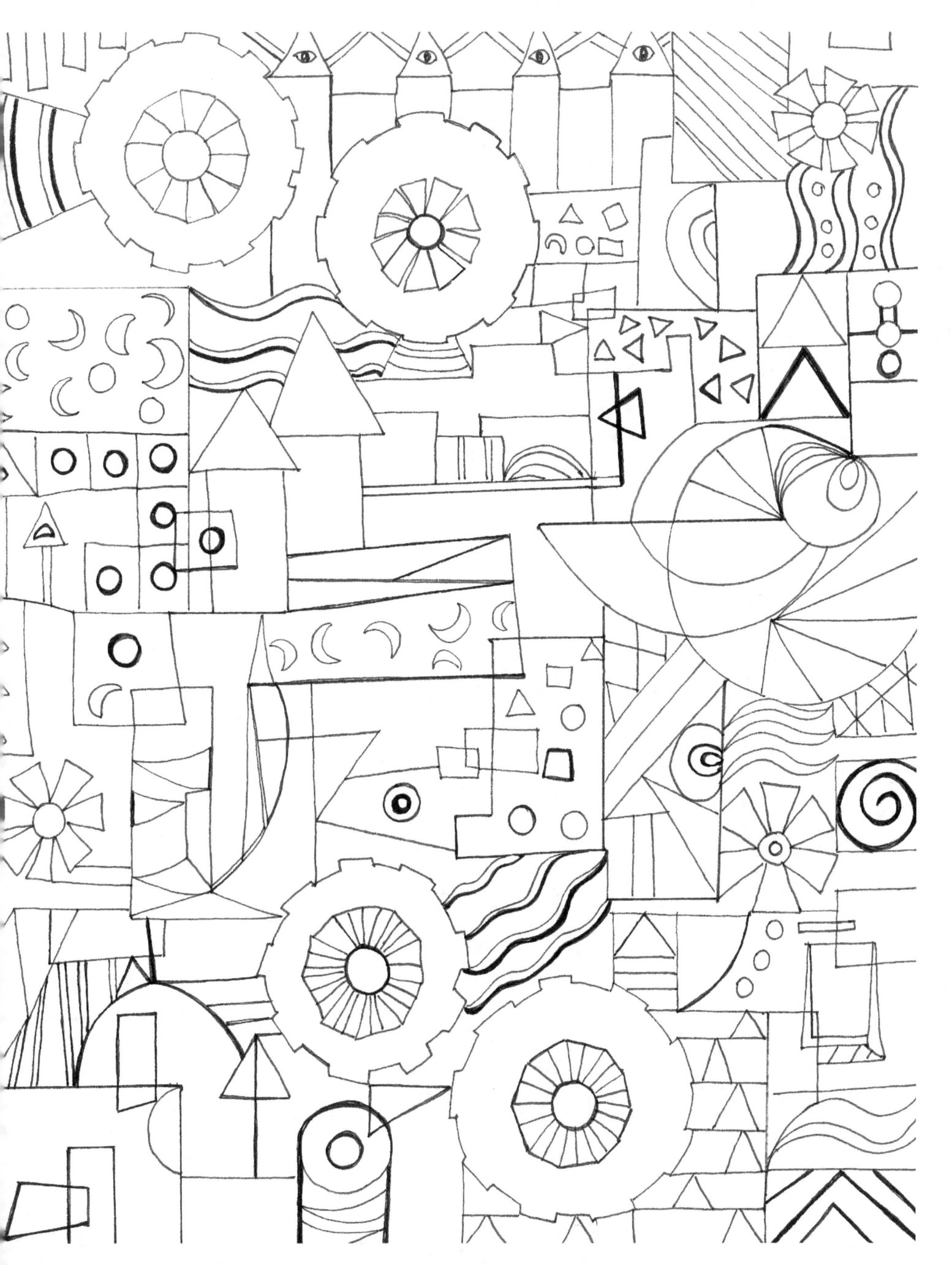

fortunate is he who does not carry envy as a companion
Rumi

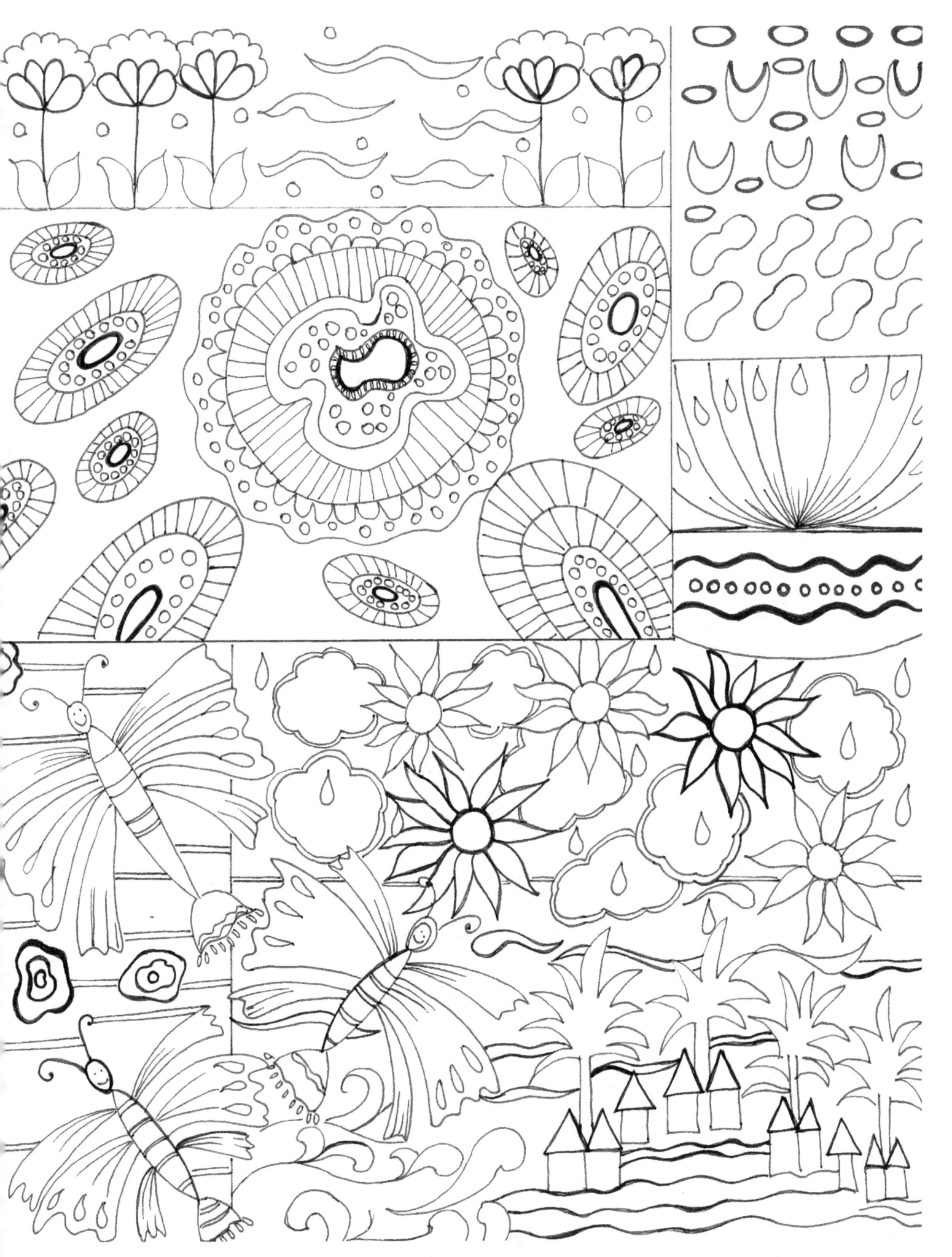

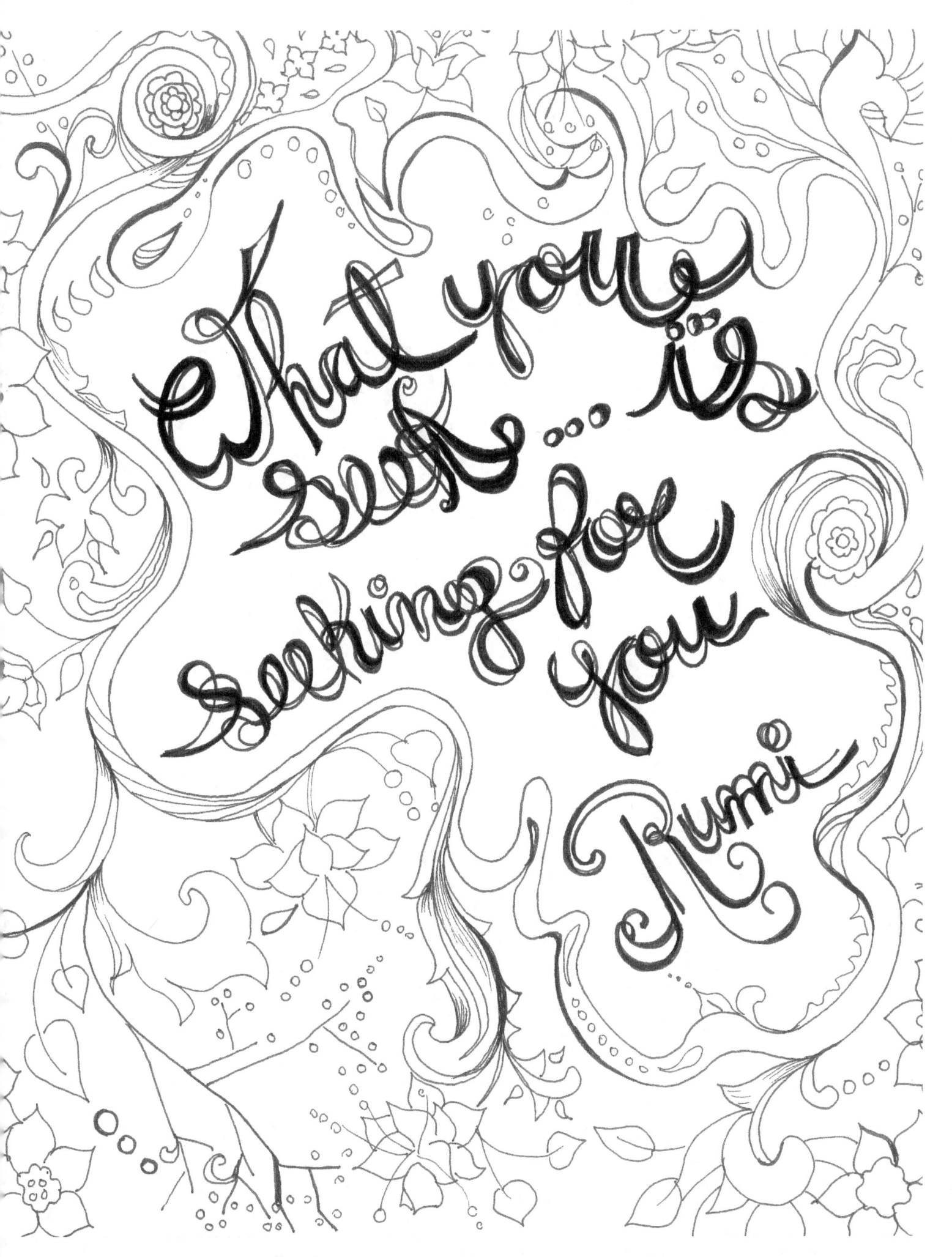

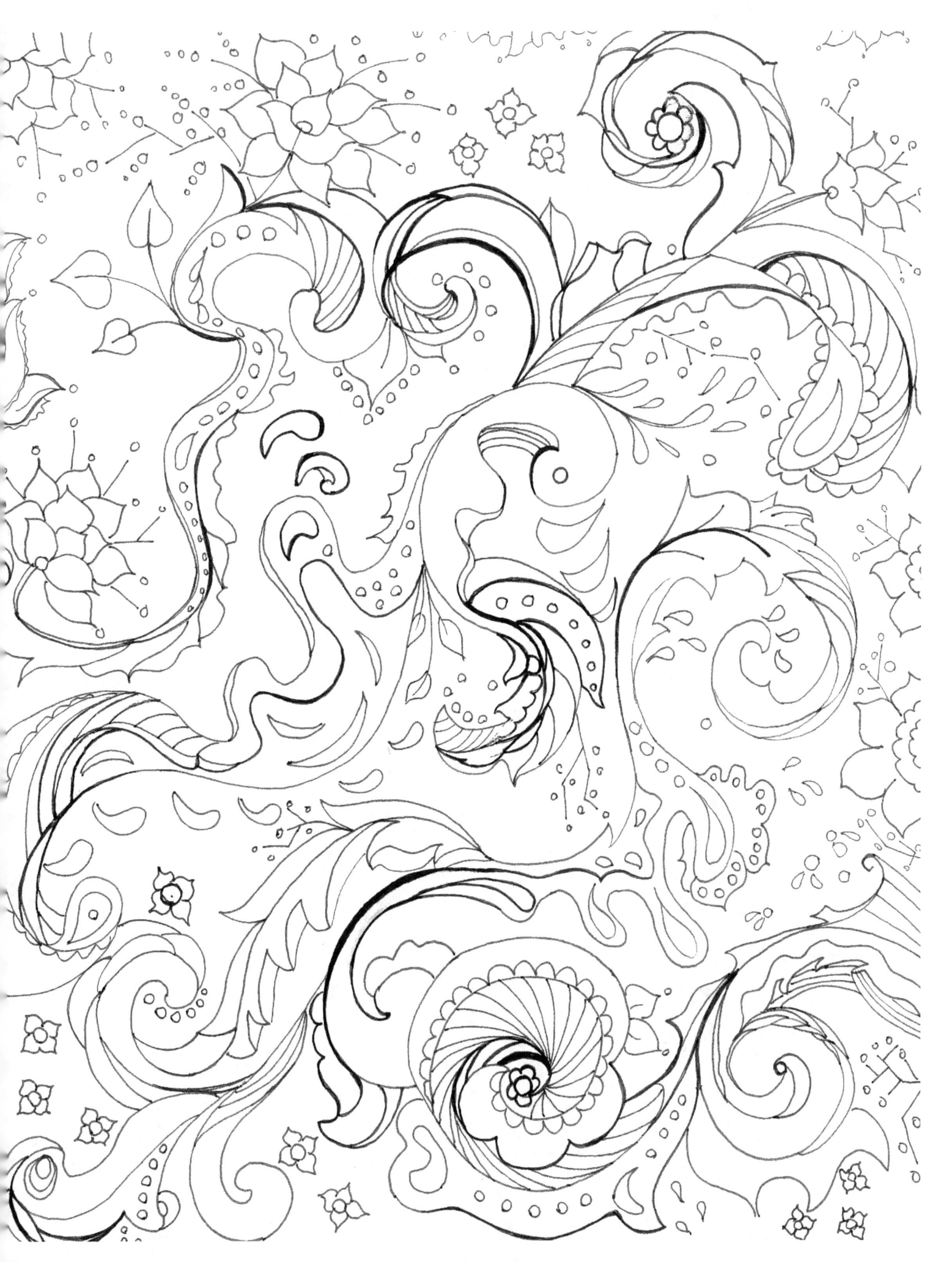

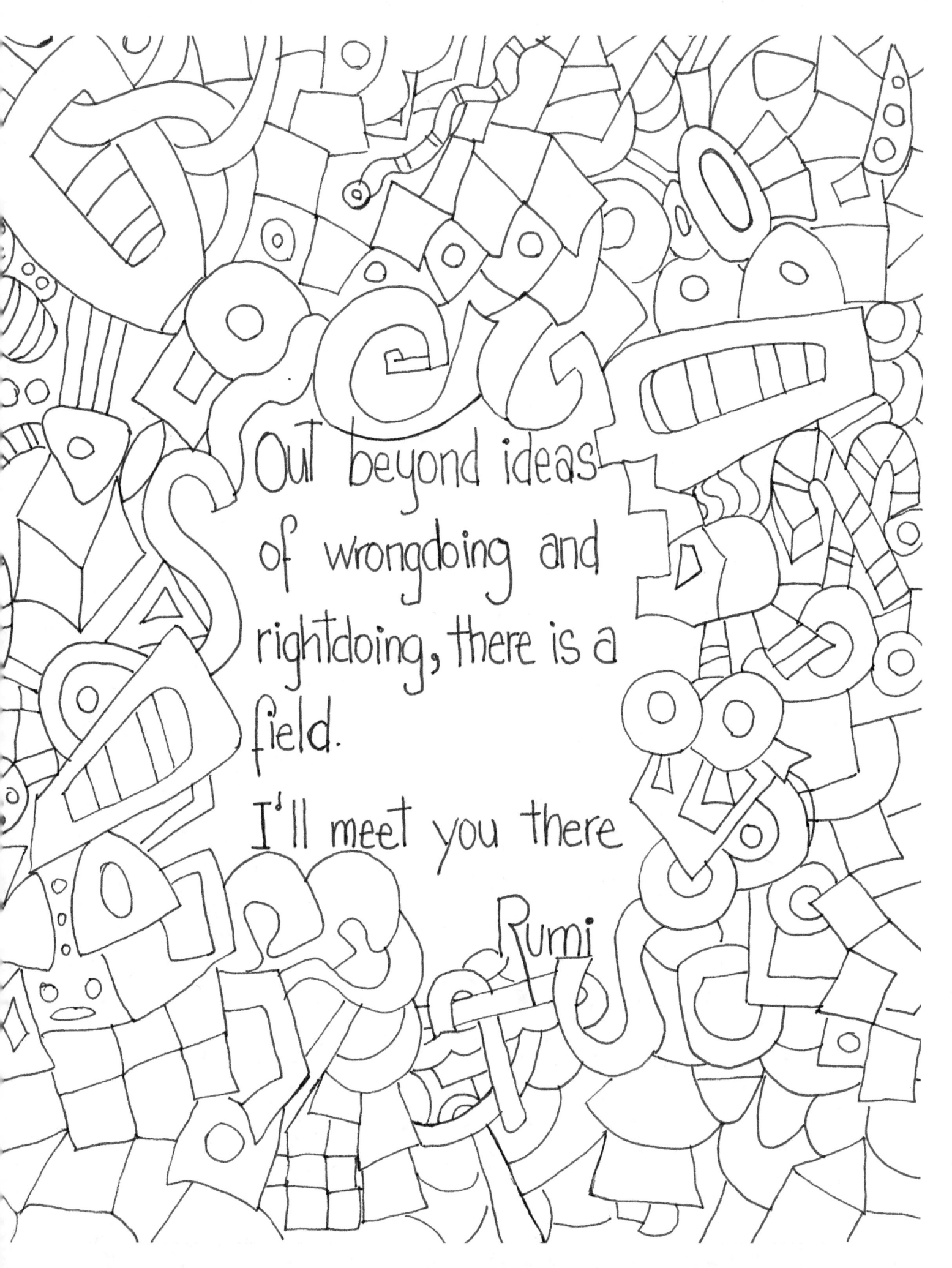

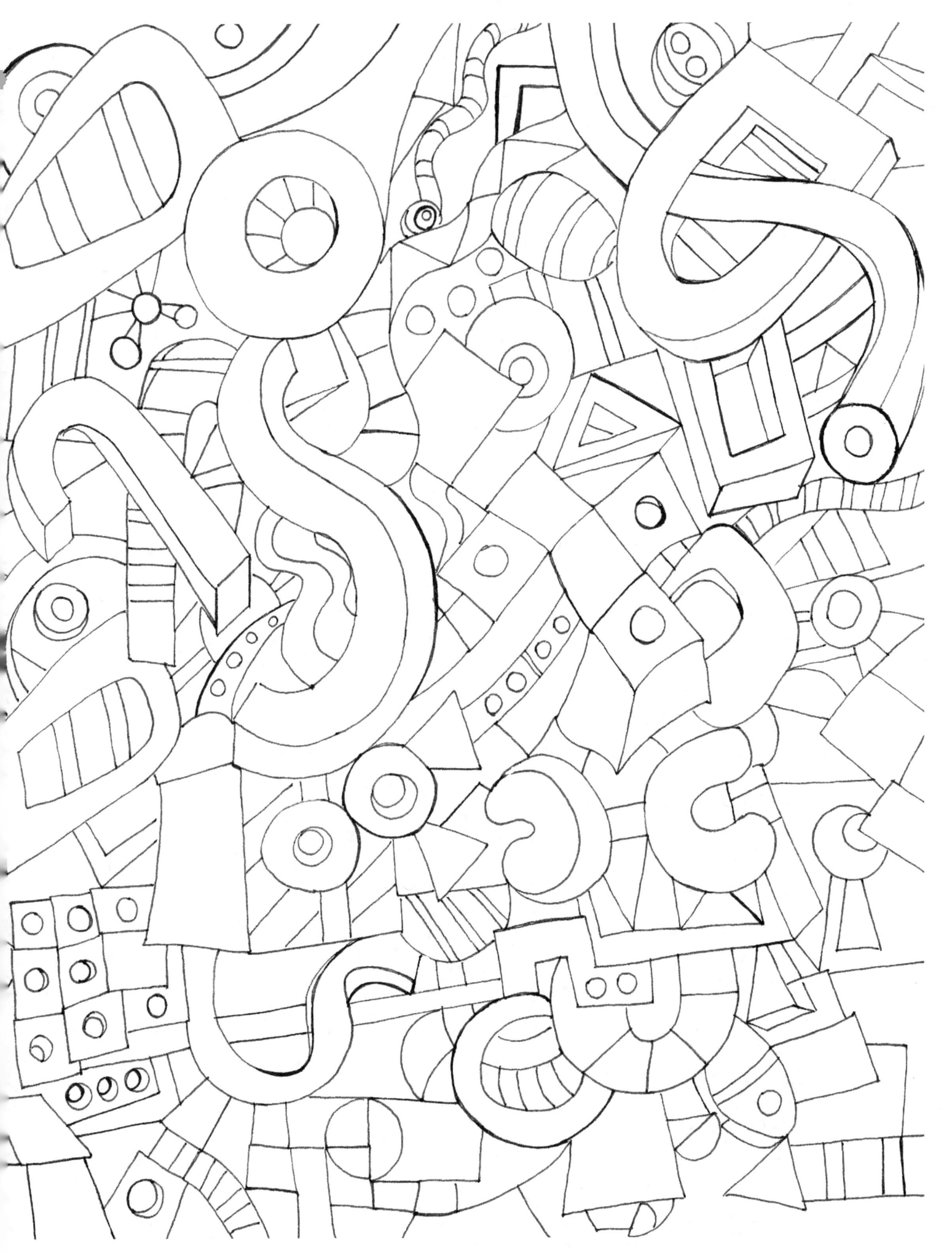

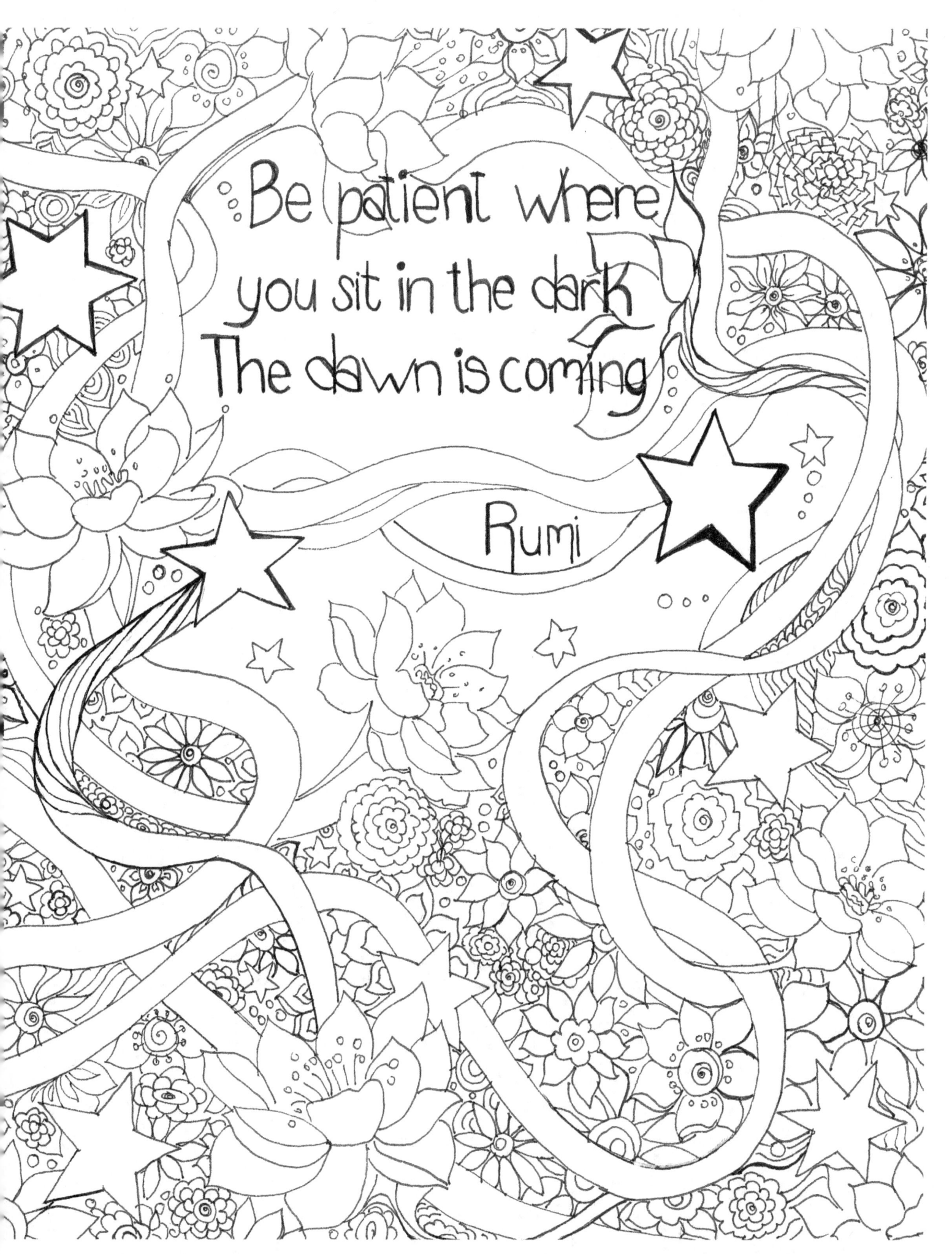

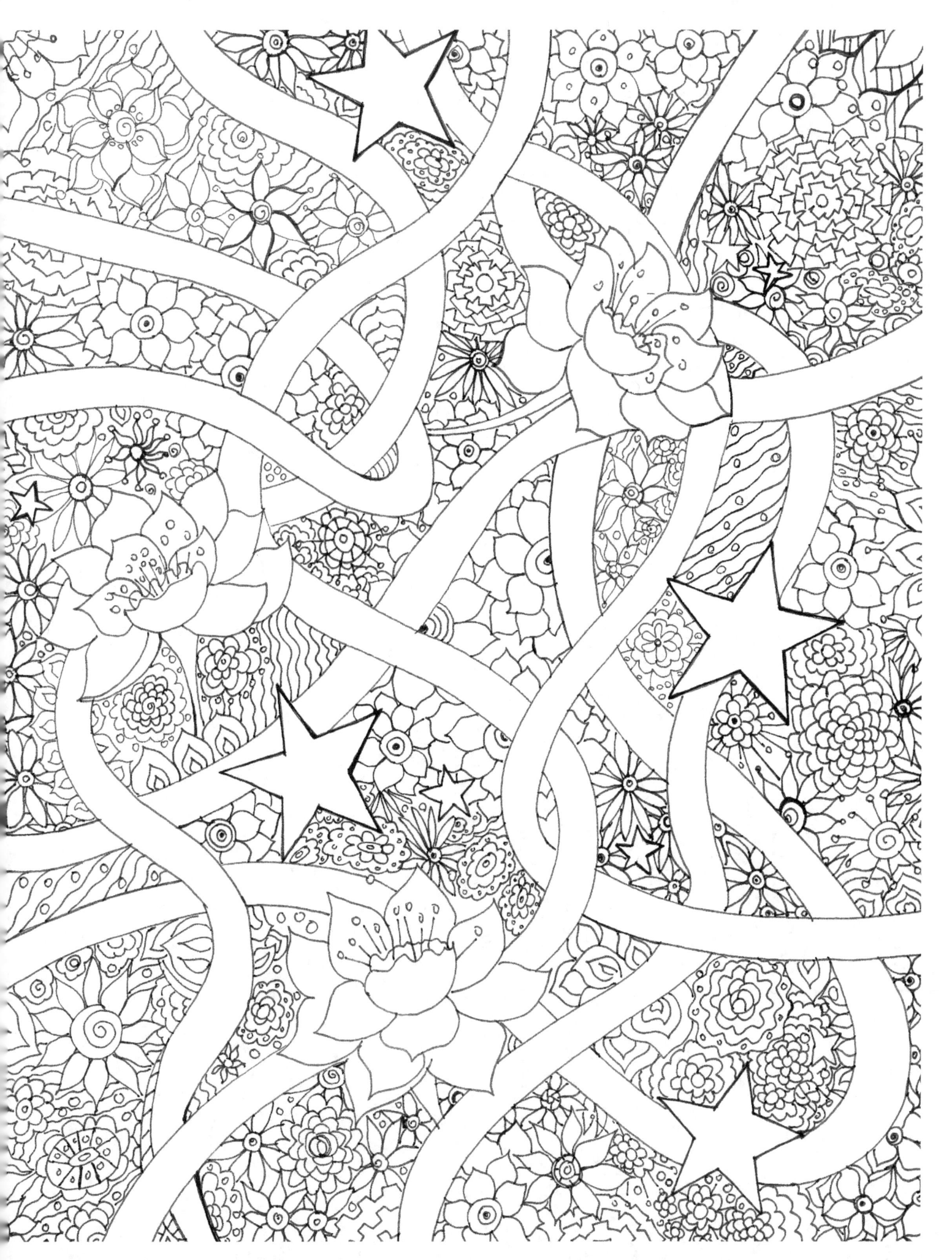

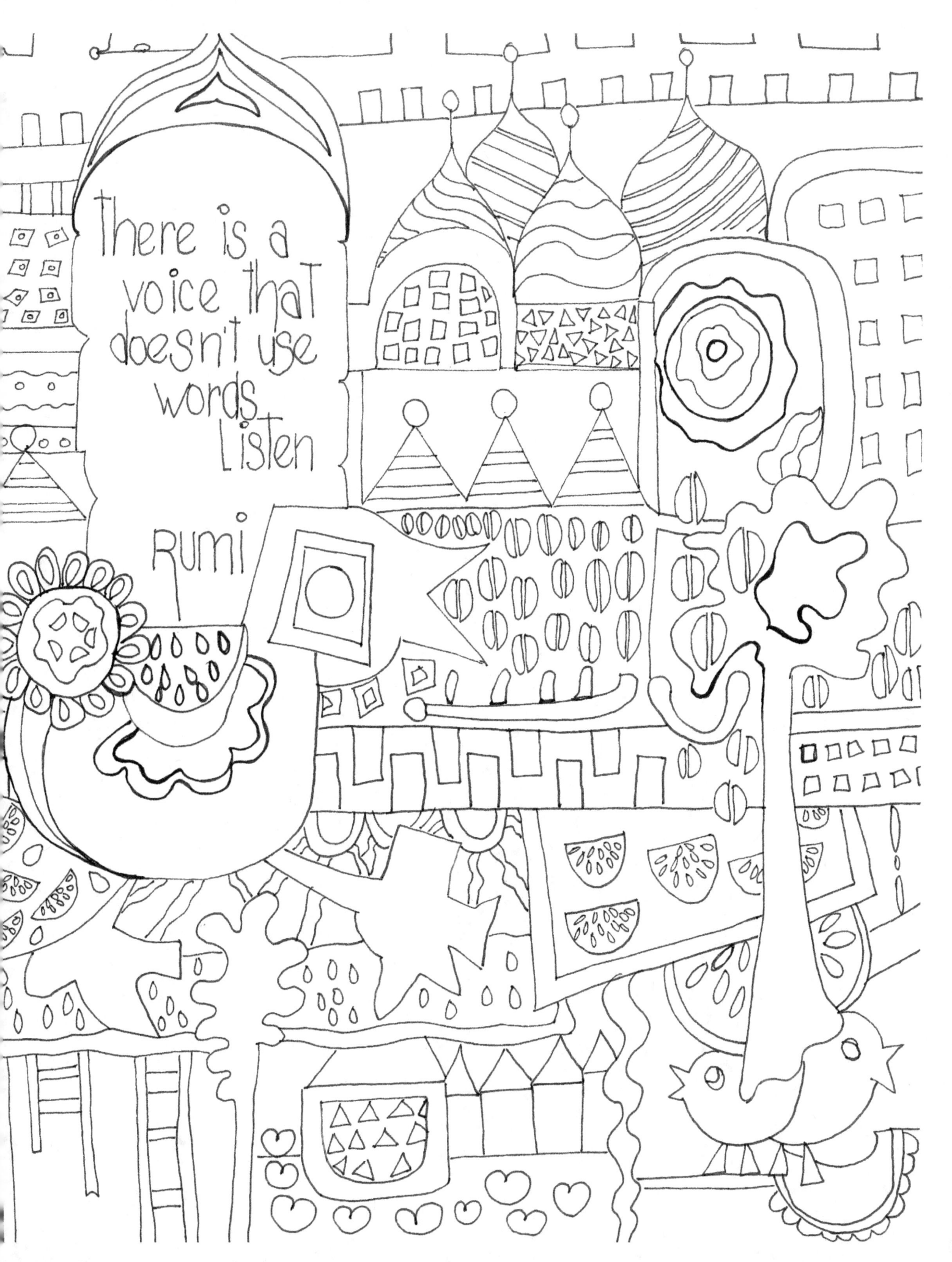

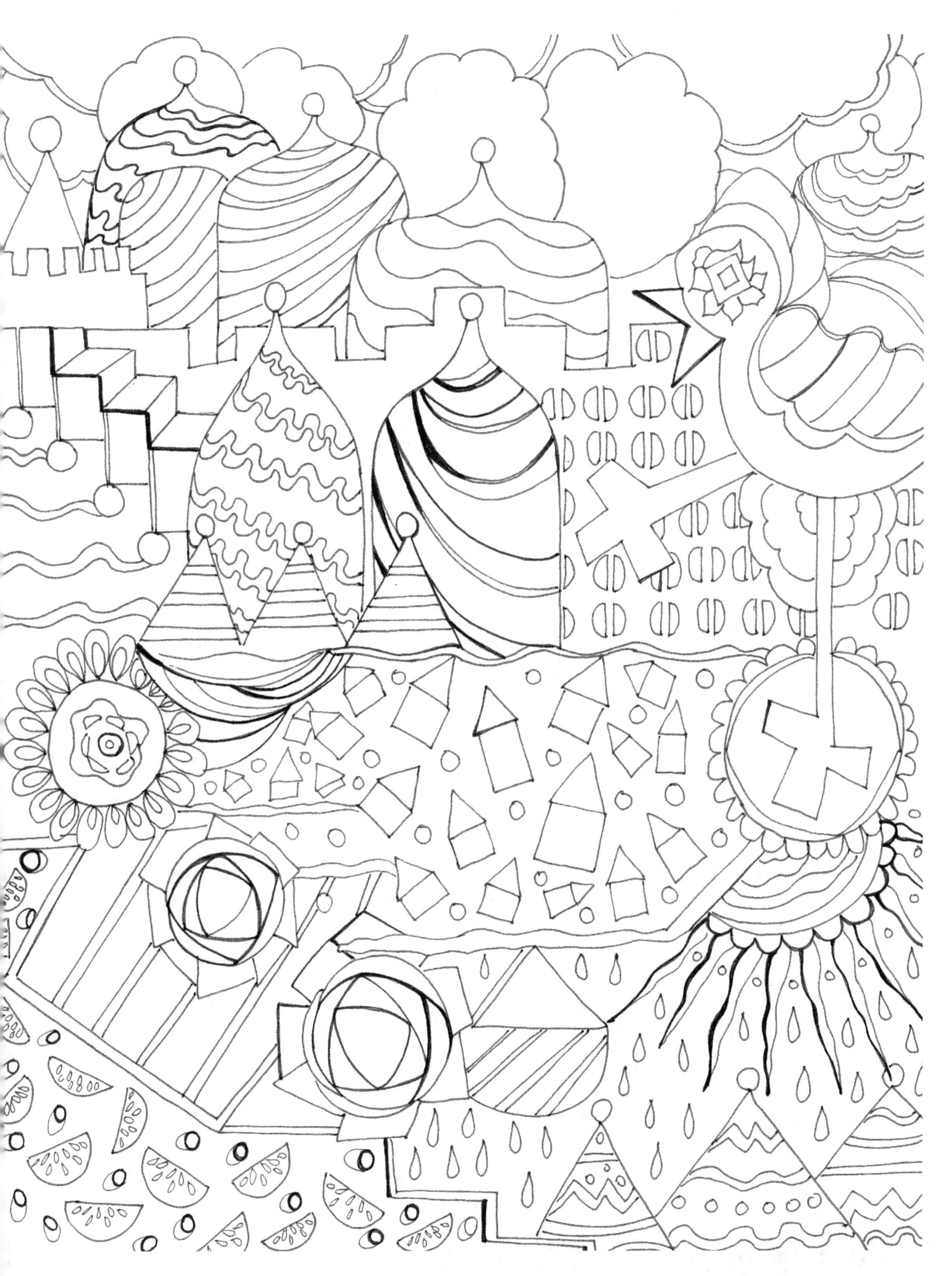